Norfolk
Remembered

The Author.   (Photo by courtesy of *Eastern Daily Press*)

Norfolk Remembered

by

Robert Bagshaw

By the Same Author:
Poppies to Paston
Toothy Goes to War

ISBN   Hardback: 0 900616 29 6
        Paperback: 0 900616 30 X

        Printed and published by
        Geo. R. Reeve Ltd., Damgate, Wymondham, Norfolk

Contents

Illustrations

Acknowledgements

This book owes much to the many old friends who have so willingly shared both memories and photographs with me. Those in the first group are too numerous to mention, but for assistance with illustrations I am particularly indebted to Bridget Belson, Rhoda Bunn, Amy Elizabeth Chamberlin, "Shrimp" Davies, Brian Hedge, Mike Ling, Diana Rollason, Philip Standley, Clifford Temple, Beryl Tooley, Norman Trollor and Roy Worton.

I am also grateful to my more recently acquired friends at BBC Radio Norfolk for the warmth of their welcome on so many Tuesday afternoons. In particular, I thank Keith Skipper for his friendly encouragement and, furthermore, for his very generous foreword to this book.

Bob Bagshaw.
Wymondham.
October 1989.

FOREWORD

by Keith Skipper

Bob is the third member of the Bagshaw brotherhood with whom I have enjoyed a fruitful relationship.

I first encountered the family in 1962 when Stanley, by common consent the brightest star in the Bagshaw constellation, had the good sense to encourage my journalistic ambitions. He was editor-in-chief of the Norfolk News Company – now Eastern Counties Newspapers – and I was taken on as a junior reporter on leaving school after my interview in the room where big decisions were made in Redwell Street, Norwich.

I met Peter Bagshaw a few years later at the Yarmouth office of the local press empire. He worked upstairs on the "Eastern Daily Press", while I joined the weekly ranks on the "Mercury" below. He was a delightful colleague and friend, full of homely support for an innocent abroad in my early days by the sea, and blessed with a twinkling sense of humour that shone through the dullest of routine tasks. We often sat next to each other at committee and council meetings, at dinners and in court. Peter's droll observations and endless anecdotes broke the monotony on many occasions when I wondered if his brother Stanley had really done me a good turn after all. Stanley and Peter have gone, countless proud editions behind them, but the family flair for the written word is in excellent hands.

I had to wait until 1986 for my introduction to Bob Bagshaw. He came to BBC Radio Norfolk and the Dinnertime Show for a chat about his book, Poppies to Paston, the story of his Norfolk childhood. Perhaps my liberal praise for his brothers acted as a spur, but it soon became clear that a top-class mardler was waiting for proper recognition alongside a writer of considerable appeal.

Bob duly accepted the invitation to drop in every fortnight after two o'clock on a Tuesday to tell a few tales with a local flavour. Indeed, the seeds for this splendid volume germinated as his studio visits attracted more and more interest. "So much material here, I'll never get it all in today" he sighed as the letters multiplied and the memories flowed after a few telling instalments. I urged him to savour his new-found popularity on the wireless, and I was convinced he would find time eventually to fashion all that material into a book.

Here it is, a Norfolk volume to underline Bob's deep affection for the county as he introduces some of the faces and places he has met on his way since early days at Cromer. Many of the characters demand a spot through the very nature of their exploits – legendary lifeboatman Henry Blogg and the great naturalist Arthur Patterson, for example – but Bob has the happy knack of calling up some of Norfolk's lesser-known players for first-team action. He asks Dick Amis to take a bow for bringing back a truant penguin at Cromer. He salutes Lou Pestell, a woman who forsook the comforts and convention of a good home for a life on the open road. He pushes forward Gilly Hewitt, a fishing fanatic and one of those people who could make life seem better by his mere presence. He still wonders how Norman Trollor managed to keep two cinemas going by virtue of a 1915 belt-driven Douglas motor bike.

Bob rests a light hand on the shoulders of numerous old friends, often coaxing them into revelations and yarns to illuminate the passing years. You get the impression they tell Bob because they trust him . . and like him. He does not tumble into the old trap of making nostalgia dependent on mawkishness to catch the attention. On the contrary, we often get Norfolk warts and all rather than the traditional extra helpings of clinging sentimentality.

Bob is a natural communicator, both in front of a microphone and through the pages of books such as this. The fact that he digresses so easily on the air – often trying to blame others for his own happy wanderings – simply means he is destined to have more material than expected before the next programme. And for the next book. A Norfolk gift, perhaps, for turning one good yarn into a dozen, knowing full well none will be allowed to go to waste. A family trait, no doubt, to make rich capital out of the world about him. Born by the sea, raised in the country and brought into manhood in the city.

Transforming the ordinary into the exceptional is Bob Bagshaw's true talent. He has never been too busy reaching for the stars so as to fail to notice the flowers at his feet. Here he weaves them into a garland worthy of crowning the broadest Norfolk smile.

CHAPTER 1

The Good Old Days?

"It was the best of times, it was the worst of times . . . it was the season of Light, it was the season of Darkness . . . it was the spring of hope, it was the winter of despair". I suppose I should apologise to Charles Dickens for borrowing the opening lines of his "Tale of Two Cities", but somehow they seem strangely appropriate to those early days of the present century when we were busy growing up in the countryside of Norfolk.

Memories are tantalising things. They haunt us and humour us and often, if we are not careful, they try to cheat the present by glorifying the past. The days in which we live give us everything that is in them, be it good or bad. Our memory of past days tends to preserve only the best, while the worst slips back into the shadows. Thus it is that those of us who look back with affection at "the good old days" often stand accused of wearing rose-tinted spectacles. But such an accusation is unjust, for there are aspects of life in those early days which even the quirks of memory cannot erase.

I remember children with rickets and others, born with some mental deficiency, being "put away". On a more modest scale I recall spending long hours sitting in my pushchair in the yard around the gasworks where my mother, in common with all the women of her time, believed that the fumes would cure whooping cough. I remember the hunger marchers and the many men who worked for a mere pittance without complaint, lest they should lose their jobs.

But I also remember the days when women could walk alone in the streets without constant fear of attack and when there was no need to tell children not to talk to strangers. They were the days when nobody felt it necessary to lock up their houses, irrespective of how long they were out, and when life went on at a more leisurely pace. There was peace and, above all, contentment.

Perhaps we were fortunate in being countryfolk rather than having to live our lives in the dirt and grime of some large city, for it was the land and what it produced that set the pattern of our existence. It was a time when Norfolk was truly rural and when farming was a way of life rather than the major industry it has now become. Much of our food came straight from the land. Our milk, straight from the cow, was poured into jugs which stood on the larder shelves wearing white net covers weighted with coloured glass beads. Our butter, with a rich creaminess which would make present-day medical experts cringe, was spread thickly on freshly-cut bread, still warm from the bakehouse oven.

But all this, of course, was at the mercy of the weather, and I well recall one incident involving old Ezra Childerhouse, who had a farm down by the Common. I was rather fond of Mr. Childerhouse, for I had a feeling that he liked me and, after all, what little boy can resist being liked? For a long time the weather had been wonderful for picnics in the woods and cricket on the Common, but everything in the fields was dying of thirst. On this particular evening I was in one of the barns with "Smiler" Storey, so-named because of his permanent ear-to-ear grin, rather like the letter U. Suddenly, the sky began to darken and the heavens opened up and sent rain hurtling down in torrents. Within minutes we heard a man shouting and, as we looked into the yard, there was the figure of Mr. Childerhouse, arms raised to the heavens, crying "It's come! It's come!" It was a shout of gratitude to God and it seemed an eternity that he stood there, his bare head dripping, his open shirt becoming soaked and tears of joy running down his cheeks.

It was at harvest time that the weather played a vital part, for the gathering in of the corn was a long and arduous process which involved the entire community. Nowadays, the state of mechanisation on our farms is such that, once the combines move in, the whole process is completed in a matter of days. No longer do we hear the sound of scythe on whetstone; no longer can we enjoy the spectacle of working horses plodding majestically round the shimmering corn as the blades of the cutter steadily reduce the crop to an ever-diminishing rectangle in the centre of the field. No longer can our noses savour that mixed smell of burnt hoof, hot metal and steam which used to filter out of the local blacksmith's forge – unless it be where somebody now keeps horses out of love for the animal rather than necessity. In my boyhood, however, the horse still reigned supreme and it was he who set the pace. Women and children played their part, not only by taking refreshment for the men when they took their short breaks for "elevenses" and "fourses", but also by acting as "stookers". Setting up the sheaves

Milk in the can from Worstead.

in clumps to dry in the sun, they slowly but surely drew the traditional picture of extended rows across the length of the field. The harvester's day was long and hard, and yet there was a certain touch of romance about it. There is nothing romantic about a combine-harvester spouting dust or a modern baler spitting out straw bales like monster bricks.

The harvest field used to be a haven of delight for youngsters and, strangely enough, it seems, in retrospect, to have been much more tranquil. Now, however, it is no fit playground for the young, who will never know the excitement of chasing rabbits across the stubble, of riding on the loaded wagon as it bumps from field to yard or, the biggest thrill of all, being "howdgee boy" for the day and sitting astride the massive horse that pulled the wagon.

The age-old tradition of the Harvest Supper was going into decline, but the farm worker could still find relief from his labours in the local hostelry, for there were very few parishes which did not boast at least one public house. Some of them, with their wooden benches and bare floors (often liberally sprinkled with sand), were hardly havens of comfort, but this in no way diminished the pleasure of a quiet mardle over a pint of ale. Then, by way of

The horse dictated the pace of our lives.

"Fourses" at Frogmoor Farm, Briston.

Children's rides came in many forms.

The Village Forge, Poringland.

The Quoits team at Briston "Horseshoes" (now the "John H. Stracey") c.1922.

diversion, there were always darts, dominoes and the traditional pub game of quoits.

Holidays were both infrequent and brief, but our year was liberally sprinkled with festive days which were highlights of the country year. There were still some parishes where, on the first Monday after Twelfth Day, the plough was taken to be blessed at the local church; and May Day really was the first day of May rather than the political holiday it has now become. Out came the maypole, and round it danced the children, with the Queen of the May, "the fairest maid in the village", presiding over the whole affair. Rogation Week was also the time for the traditional ceremony of "beating the bounds", when the elders of the church would lead the children around the boundaries of the parish in a tradition which stemmed from the days before such things as title deeds and ordnance survey. The fourth Sunday in Lent had long been a special day, for it was Mothering Sunday. Nowadays we have Mother's Day, but Mothering Sunday was very different. It was the one day of the year when girls and boys who lived away "in service" in the big houses and on the farms were allowed to go home and be reunited with their parents. The presents they took

Maypole dancing at Aylsham, 1906.

Beating the bounds at Holt, c. 1906.

were simple things such as samplers or embroidered chair covers which they had made, and the flowers were more likely the wild ones which they gathered as they made their way home across the fields.

One of the big events of the year was the annual fête, although we rarely referred to it by that name, for it was a French word which had not fully found its way into our vocabulary. At Bacton it was the Whit Monday Frolic, where the huge urn (which, I am happy to learn, still survives) steadily churned out vast quantities of steaming hot tea and where the star turn was always Percy Pigg, the local exponent of step dancing. Potter Heigham, too, had its step dancer in the form of Harry Cox, who was also a renowned folk singer, and, of course, there was the immortal Sidney Grapes. Swanton Abbot Gala was a wonderful example of co-operation, for it was a four-parish affair involving also the adjoining villages of Westwick, Skeyton and Scottow. There was little need for a celebrity opener, for most of the combined twelve hundred population of the parishes were there at the start and stayed till the end. Most of the attractions were of a simplicity which reflected the lifestyle of the period, but it is surprising how many of them involved the use of a greasy pole. There was pillow fighting on the pole, the pillows being merely sacks packed with straw. There was a vertical pole, again well greased, up which contestants were challenged to climb in order to win the pig which was secured on top. To take things to the extreme, they even had a greasy pig waiting in an enclosure to be caught. It must have been a hard day for the poor pig, and the clothing worn by the contestants must surely have suffered in all these activities, for everybody dressed up to attend the Gala.

Evening entertainment was of a similarly undemanding nature, with silent films at the Picturedrome at North Walsham being the highlight of the week. For live shows there were such places as the Corn Hall and the Salvation Army Hall, but the scene of my greatest memories was the Church Rooms which had earlier been a theatre and then the town's first Penny School. It was there that I made my first public appearance, playing the unlikely role of an owl in a nativity play, and it was there also that Herbert Ribbons (of whom we shall hear more later) unwittingly gained the loudest applause of the night. A professional conjurer from Norwich had been engaged to raise the standard of a certain evening's entertainment and, for half an hour or so, he had held us spellbound. Then,

Swanton Abbot Gala.

coming down among the audience, he stood against old Herbert and addressed us with the words: "Now, ladies and gentlemen, I shall proceed to amaze you by producing a live rabbit from the pocket of this man's jacket". "I doubt that, master", said Herbert. "I've got a ferret in there already".

It was in the midst of this unpretentious lifestyle that we of the younger generation received our early education at the Council School. There we learned to add and subtract, to express ourselves in reasonable English and, above all, to become responsible members of society. I suppose most of our teachers could hardly be described as being the top fruit of the educational tree, but they were typical of the caring community in which we had the good fortune to spend our early years.

At certain times in the year our schooling was interrupted in order that matters of health could be attended to. There were, for instance, the times when the white-clad figure of the "nit nurse" would arrive and rummage through our hair in search of un-welcome creepy-crawlies. Her presence in our midst gave little cause for concern, our only worry being that, in the course of her ministrations, she might spread the infestation from unhealthy heads to those of us who had previously been unaffected. In any case, getting rid of the insect invaders presented no great problem, for it merely meant a trip to the chemist for a ha'porth of quassia chips. Quassia is a South American wood which, when cut into small pieces and steeped in boiling water, produces a liquid which is lethal to headlice. It was just one of the many natural remedies which were in common use in those days and which I firmly believe were superior to many modern drugs. In the first place, they were inexpensive and, furthermore, we never had to worry about such things as "side effects".

Though we had no great fear of the nit nurse, the same could not be said of Mr. Millican, for he was the school dentist. It was not the man himself that we feared, for he was of a very friendly disposition, but we all dreaded our enforced entry into the "chamber of horrors" in which he dealt with our dental imperfections. We were never given any advance warning of his impending arrival, for to have done so would inevitably have led to a marked increase in truancy. The first indication we received of what lay in store for us was when we arrived at school and found his dreaded caravan parked in the playground. There followed a period of perhaps a week in which any form of concentration on lessons was out of the question. In the first place, there was our steady procession into Mr. Millican's chair for his assessment of the situation. Then came the apprehensive wait to see which of us would receive one of those slips of paper which had to be taken home and signed by one of our parents to give him permission to proceed. Those of us unfortunate enough to come into that category studied the form in great detail in an effort to discover what torture lay ahead, but we could never understand his writing.

Even for those of us whose Ivory Castles were found to be free of imperfections, the next few days were not without a certain degree of tension, for it was impossible not to feel sympathy for our more unfortunate classmates. A glance through the window would reveal the figure of a friend timidly climbing the steps into the caravan and then, after what seemed an interminable wait, he would emerge and stagger back to the classroom with his mouth packed with bloodstained cotton wool and a look of assumed heroism on his face. It was always a happy day when Mr. Millican packed up his instruments and trundled off down the road in search of his next batch of unsuspecting victims.

One of the great events of our childhood summers was the Annual Sunday School Treat. It was an affair of utter simplicity,

20

School Treat Wagon at Wells.

but we looked forward to it with eager anticipation as the great day approached. Then we would gather at the appointed place where a farm wagon, pulled by two horses, would carry us away for a day of bliss. First, however, there was the little matter of popping into the church or chapel for a few prayers to ensure that our trip would be blessed with good fortune. One of the prayers was a request that our intended location might be blessed with fine weather, and there were times when, in our impatience, we felt sure that, if the preacher didn't get a move on, it would be raining before we got there. Eventually we would emerge and, clutching the orange, the apple and the bag of sweets which we had each been given, we would climb aboard the wagon.

It was a scene which was repeated in every parish throughout the kingdom in those halcyon days of summer, for the school treat was always a great day in the country calendar. For many inland youngsters it gave the promise of a day at the seaside, and places like Wells were regularly subjected to invasion by hordes of excited urchins. Indeed, almost every Saturday in summer would find Abraham's Bosom at that resort providing parking spaces for the assortment of farm vehicles which, having deposited their human cargoes, stood patiently awaiting the return trip. For those of us in Cromer, however, the beach was no great attraction, and our trip took us inland, though we did not venture very far afield. Usually we headed for the woods at Felbrigg Hall, sometimes to Roman Camp or, when we were very adventurous, we might get as far as Pretty Corner. There we would engage in games and races until, tired out but deliriously happy, we would climb back into the wagon for the lazy journey home.

In most cases the day passed by without untoward incident, but Stanley Sergent recalls one occasion when an extra element of excitement was injected into the proceedings. They were on their way to Felbrigg and the pair of sturdy horses had made gallant progress up the hill when, having just passed Cromer Hall, there came the sound of a tremendous crack and the wagon lurched to one side. The metal tyre had come adrift from one of the wheels, with the result that the wheel had broken, tipping the wagon over and depositing the young passengers in a heap on the road. Fortunately none of them suffered serious injury, but there then followed a long wait by the roadside while a new wheel was obtained and fitted so that the journey could be resumed. It seems most probable that they would have reached their destination more quickly if they had picked themselves up and walked the rest of the way. But, of course, it wouldn't have been half the fun.

During all the enjoyment of those happy school treat days there was one young lad who never took part. He came from what would now be called a deprived background and he certainly had no religious affiliations. Thus he was not able to join us, and he would enviously watch as each successive cartload of children made its way out of the town. Eventually, after much consideration, he decided that it would be worth joining a Sunday School in order that he could go on one of these treats, and so it was that, for the first time, he found his way into the chapel of his choice. Almost immediately, however, he faced a great disappointment, for he had thought that all he had to do was to get his name entered in the register and he would automatically go on the treat. It came as quite a shock when he discovered that, in order to qualify, it was necessary for him to obtain attendance marks on a specified number of Sundays during the year. The number varied with different churches, some requiring a dozen and others as many as fifteen or sixteen. This was a bitter blow, but he thought that, as he had started, he might as well carry on. Then his little mind got busy (he was quite a bright young lad) and he realised that, if he worked things out carefully, he could qualify for more than one outing by joining other Sunday Schools. There were four at that time and he knew full well that he could not qualify for all of them, for there were just not enough Sundays in a year. By organising his activities with great care, however, and alternating his attendances, he realised that it was possible to qualify for three of them, and that is what he proceeded to do. Thus it was that, on three successive Saturdays in the summer, he was amongst the crowd of children happily crowding into the farm wagon and being transported up the hill to Felbrigg and Roman Camp.

I have no knowledge as to whether, as a result, he was converted to the idea of Christianity, but he was certainly all in favour of School Treats. Indeed, the whole business had taken such a hold on him that, on the day when the fourth outing was to take place, he was unable to resist going down to see them off. There was the same old cart with the two horses and the children clambering aboard and getting ready to set off. There was only one slight difference from the previous weeks, and this was that the cart had a different driver. Indeed, not only was he different, but he was also not a local man, and he was loudly proclaiming the fact that he didn't know the way.

Hearing this, our little friend on the side of the road called out, "I know the way, mister. I can show you".

"Can you, my boy?" said the driver. "Right you are, then. You hop up here alongside o' me."

Without a second's hesitation, the lad was up there sitting beside the driver, and thus it was that he achieved the impossible by going on all four Sunday School Treats.

A certain worthy writer, whose name escapes me, once said: "Man is always so busy reaching for the stars that he fails to notice the flowers at his feet". Throughout my years, a vast number of ordinary Norfolk folk have woven themselves inextricably into my life, playing parts of which they themselves were largely unaware. They were the flowers at my feet and now, in the pages which follow, they have become the stars, for this is a book about people.

But we must go back to the beginning, and that means Cromer, for it was there, in that little room above the Press Office, that I first saw the light of day.

CHAPTER 2

Cromer Beginnings.

"You must take us as you find us". That endearing little phrase which, for so long, has accompanied an invitation to visit a Norfolk homestead, gives a most penetrating insight into the character of the folk who have traditionally inhabited this county of ours. It is the native's way of assuring the prospective visitor of a warm welcome — as long as the visitor recognises his host's right to make changes to his way of life only when he himself considers it desirable. The newcomer who overlooks the "terms and conditions" runs the risk of being received with something less than enthusiasm. He who accepts them, however, will quickly become one of the family.

I believe it to be this very characteristic which has enabled Cromer to retain the charm which attracted the first visitors two hundred years ago. Having been born in the town, I suppose I must admit to a certain degree of bias, but I believe that the great attraction which it still has for visitors stems from the fact that it has never tried to be anything but itself. It has never wanted to become another Yarmouth or Blackpool. It has never felt the urge to build itself a Tower Ballroom or to turn its Golden Mile into an endless succession of pintable saloons and bingo halls. This is not to suggest that Cromer has never done anything to attract visitors. Indeed, the reverse is very much the case, for both the town and its people have gone to great lengths to provide memorable holidays for visitors. The most striking feature of the wide range of attractions which has been made available, however, is that, for the most part, they have always been in keeping with the character and traditions of the town. It is, in fact, almost as though, for the past two centuries, Cromer has been saying to the outside world, "We'd love you to come and stay with us – but you must take us as you find us".

In the beginning, of course, it was not too difficult to make visitors happy, for Cromer's fame began as a health resort. The climate was the great attraction and their ideas of entertainment were modest in the extreme. A walk along the promenade, an afternoon on the beach and an evening stroll along the cliffs just about summed up the days activities, and everybody was happy. It was as early as the end of the eighteenth century that the delights of Cromer had been discovered, but they were not available to the masses because of the difficulties of travel. It was a cluster of local County families who set the ball rolling, notably the Gurneys of Earlham and the Barclays of Northrepps Hall. In view of the fact that the two families boasted some thirty children between them, it seems likely that the beach may have been the main attraction. Other families later joined them and soon Cromer could boast of some of the enticements of the inland spas, with a Bath House for salt water immersion and a Subscription Room for reading and various social activities. Still it was the climatic conditions which beckoned visitors and, in 1904, the "Daily News" was moved to declare that "For robust mortals wishful to be even more robust, Cromer is the place . . . . Your lungs are strengthened by air blowing pure and unadulterated from the North Pole". In today's centrally-heated society one cannot think that the local tourist authority would welcome such a recommendation, although the writer did add that "the Cromer sunshine will bring out all your freckles".

It has often been said that it was Clement Scott who was responsible for putting Cromer on the map as a holiday resort, but I believe this to be only partly true. Certainly his writings brought the attractions of the area to the attention of a wider public, but it was the laying of the railway line in 1882 which made it possible for people to get there. It was, indeed, the railway which had carried him to the town in order that he might describe the pleasures of the district to readers of the "Daily Telegraph". Furthermore, he did not much like the place. It was its lack of appeal for him, in fact, which led him to take that fateful stroll over the cliffs to Beckhythe, as Overstrand was then known, and to the beginning of his long-lasting love affair with Poppyland. It was his preference for Beckhythe which, on every New Year's Eve for the next fifteen years, led him on his ritual walk up Tower Lane to see the New Year in from the Garden of Sleep.

In later years, Scott was moved to express regret at the rapid changes which had altered the face of Poppyland, for which he felt partly responsible. He need have had no such feeling of guilt, however, for the people wanted to go to Cromer and the town welcomed them with open arms. Up went the lavish hotels and the streets of boarding houses which were to completely transform the

Cromer from the East Cliff

26

physical structure of the place. No longer would Cromer be just a sleepy little fishing village. A new industry had been born.

Apart from providing accommodation for the visiting hordes, however, there was little else that the townsfolk needed to do, for the people found their pleasures in simple activities. In 1886 Clement Scott wrote: "Custom had established a certain fashion at this pretty little watering-place and it was religiously obeyed; it was the rule to go on the sands in the morning, to walk on one cliff for a mile in the afternoon, to take another mile in the other direction at sunset and to crowd upon the little pier at night". They were certainly not hard to please!

In the same book he even deemed it worthwhile to describe to his readers, with an almost childlike simplicity, the joys of paddling: "Paddling consists of skirting the fringe or margin of the sea with naked feet, and the pleasure is derived from the wavelets at low tide breaking upon the lower extremities, relieved from the encumbrance of shoes and stockings".

It was an age of simplicity and innocence, but one which was not destined to last for ever. Having experienced the pleasure of wavelets "breaking upon their lower extremities", the holiday-makers wished for the same sensation on their upper extremities. In other words, they wanted total immersion which, hitherto, had only been available in the privacy of the Bath House. For this to be possible without offending against the accepted standards of decency, it was necessary to find a method by means of which the prospective bather could don suitable costume prior to taking to the water and, even more to the point, remove it and get dressed afterwards. The answer, of course, was the bathing machine, a structure which always put me in mind of a kind of chicken hut on wheels. When not in use, these vehicles were parked well up the beach above the tideline and then, when required, they were pulled down to the sea by horses. Within the privacy of the machine, the bather could change into costume and then enter the sea by means of the steps which led down from the door. In common with other coastal resorts, Cromer was not slow to make these machines available and, before long, they stood in a long row all the way from the White Steps, by the Runton Road, along to the groyne near the Doctor's Steps.

The bathing machines rapidly became popular, though their use was not always without its hazards. There was one incident in particular which is still remembered with glee by older male members of the population, who are always ready to recount the details. It concerned a young lady bather who was rather late in entering the sea. Indeed, by the time she re-entered the machine in order to dry herself and don her clothing, the vehicle was almost cut off by the incoming tide. Seeing this, the proprietor rushed down with his horse and proceeded to tow the machine to safety. Unfortunately, the sudden jolt as the horse took the strain caused the young lady within to lose her balance and fall against the door. Even worse, the door, being insecurely shut, flew open and she tumbled out and fell down onto the beach. Worst of all, however, was the fact that, having removed her bathing costume, she had not a stitch of clothing with which to cover her confusion, and she rapidly became aware that a group of nearby fishermen had witnessed her mishap and were avidly absorbing the details. Her shouts to the horseman being to no avail, she had no alternative other than to chase after the rapidly receding vehicle, clamber up the steps and seek the protection of those four wooden walls.

It was an age of decorum – and of class distinction. Life was based on a set of strict rules, and everybody was required to respect the conventions of the day. This was made quite clear in an early Town Guide, which informed the reader that a keeper of the jetty and esplanade was employed "to prevent improper persons from obtruding themselves and to preserve good order. Servants in livery and all common persons are not allowed on the jetty". Furthermore, smoking was not allowed until after 9 o'clock in the evening, "at which time ladies usually retire from their evening promenade".

A charming feature of those early days was the weekly Visitors' List. On arrival in the town, visitors were invited to hand in their names and holiday addresses for inclusion on the list, thus enabling them to continue the custom of social calling which was a feature of their lives during the rest of the year. It was a facility which survived until the twenties but which faded from the scene as Cromer gradually became a mecca for the masses.

As time went by, a gradual relaxation was taking place in the conventions of the day, but this was not without its critics. Until 1898 mixed bathing was not allowed; indeed, separate areas were set aside for men and women, with a stretch of something like a hundred yards between them. Temptation can sometimes be hard to resist, however, and it was said that the speed record for the hundred yards freestyle came near to being broken on many occasions. Indeed, the situation became such that the "Cromer and North Walsham Post", reflecting the feelings of many of its readers, waged a campaign against "the lack of a sense of decency exhibited by those men and women who create a nuisance by bathing in the same area".

By the turn of the century, mixed bathing was permitted, though only between certain hours and in specified areas. Then, having attracted visitors down to the beach, Cromer proceeded to offer a host of other diversions which turned the sands into a veritable hive of activity. There were swinging boats and coconut shies, and even a gipsy caravan for fortune-telling. There were long linen lines on which bathers could hang out their costumes to dry. And, every August, there was the Annual Regatta with races for all types of sailing vessels and with the lifeboat pressed into service as the referee's launch.

The children were not forgotten for there were rides for all ages, with donkeys and ponies on the beach and, up on the Esplanade, the delightful little goat carts. They were owned by Mr. Bumfrey who lived at the top of West Street, close by the Wesleyan Chapel, and one of the young lads in charge of the vehicles was Stanley Sergent. Every day in the summer holiday he would be on duty, much to the disgust of his sister Hilda, who was inclined to the feeling that he was demeaning himself by engaging in such an activity. Indeed, it was her duty to take his tea to him every afternoon and she would go down there very surreptitiously, have a good look around to make sure nobody was watching, drop the bundle on the pavement by the side of his stand and pass on her way as though she was in no way connected with him. To be perfectly honest, I think Stanley was on a good thing, for he tells me that Mr. Bumfrey paid him ten shillings a week for his services. The only drawback from Stanley's point of view was that the goat in his charge was addicted to cigarette ends. In those days the ground was liberally sprinkled with short ends and, every time they came to one, the goat would stop, have a good sniff and then eat it. The result was that their journeys tended to become somewhat disjointed. Saturday, of course, was change-over-day, and it was then Stanley's duty to take his goat cart to certain of the hotels or boarding houses and transport luggage to Beach Station for departing holidaymakers.

It was the slightly older boys who tended to have the more difficult task of looking after the donkeys, for it is well known that they can be rather stubborn creatures. The only time when they could be relied upon to make good progress was when, at the end

Cromer Pier under construction, June 1900.

1   CROMER. — Pier and Promenade. — LL.

The Pier and Promenade, 1915.

of the day, they were turned in the direction of West Street. Then they would take off and literally scamper back to their home base.

The biggest attraction down by the beach, however, must surely have been the modern new pier, opened in 1901. It rapidly became a mecca for strollers and for those who wished to sit around the bandstand and listen to the music. This feature, however, was removed four years later and replaced with the Theatre Pavilion which, over the years, has become such a centre of entertainment. It has provided music, roller skating and well-remembered visits by a succession of concert parties. One recalls the "West End Revellers" with their comedian, Billy Seldom, and, later, the ever popular Ronnie Brandon and Dickie Pounds in "Out of the Blue". At the present time, of course, it is achieving wide acclaim as the final bastion of the tradition of end-of-the-pier shows, with an annual production well worthy of the high praise it receives.

Over the years, the area of Cromer surrounding the pier has frequently been the setting for events of high drama. Most of these concerned the activities of the lifeboat, but there were other occasions which brought local youngsters flocking to the scene. There was, for example, a period in the twenties when seaplanes became a familiar sight as they landed on the sea nearby. Indeed, they were not just ordinary seaplanes but, in fact, flying boats of the Royal Air Force. The reason for their visits is somewhat obscure, but it probably had some connection with the fact that Sir Samuel Hoare, who was Air Minister in the government at the time, had a summer residence at North Lodge on the Overstrand Road.

Even the thrill of the flying boats, however, was as nothing compared with the excitement on the day when Pip, Squeak and Wilfred came to town. Though I referred to the occasion in an earlier book, I make no apologies for returning to the subject, for I am now able to reveal the name of one of the principal characters in the drama.

We followed the adventures of the fictional animals in the pages of the "Daily Mirror" and, when we learned that they were coming to Cromer in the shape of a real live dog, penguin and rabbit, we gathered in our hundreds to see our heroes. Our little hearts pounded in unison as the three animals were paraded in front of us down by the pier but, even then, we had no idea of the drama which was about to unfold. It was Squeak, the penguin, who was the cause of all the trouble for, seeing that vast expanse of sea,

31

she decided that it was too good a chance to be missed and took off, with her minders in hot pursuit. Nothing could stop her, and she was in the water before anybody could draw near. A boat was launched, and then another and another, but Squeak was a wily old bird. She made for the water under the pier where, because of the supports, no boat could reach her.

It seemed that all would be lost, but it was then that a youthful figure emerged from the throng and began to climb along the barnacle-encrusted stanchions towards the penguin. Slowly he inched his way towards her and then, with a sweep of his arm, he gathered Squeak from the water and tucked her under his arm. The young lad who achieved this hazardous feat and brought the truant back to a hero's welcome was Dick Amis. We all cheered, and the Press cameras snapped away to provide pictures for the next day's newspapers. The "Daily Mirror", of course, made a big feature of it, and I had hoped that I might have been able to reproduce one of their photographs within these pages. Regretfully, this is not possible, but I am assured by the librarian of Mirror Group Newspapers that the events of that historic day are permanently recorded on microfilm in their London offices.

This, of course, is just as it should be, for there are many of us who still treasure memories of that historic rescue and of the young man who carried it out.

CHAPTER 3
Men of the Town

One of my earliest "friends" was an old retired fisherman who spent his days smoking his pipe and, no doubt, re-living his past as I played on the beach in my pre-school days. I think it was his never-failing kindness which attracted me, but he was also very knowledgeable about the things which I found around me, and he soon became second only to my father, in my estimation, as a fount of wisdom. He introduced me to the mysteries of barnacles and limpets and he taught me that what I called a "mermaid's purse" was really the egg-case of a dogfish. The only disappointments came in my search for unusual pebbles. I was convinced that, if I looked hard enough, I would find one which was both rare and valuable, but each little collection which I passed over for his assessment brought the same response: "Sorry, old partner. They're just ordin'ry stoons".

If the sight of my fisherman friend gave me a feeling of joy, the same could not be said for old Ben Golden, for Ben was blind and was reduced to begging in the streets. Every day he would station himself at the top of the gangway with an enamel mug at his feet to receive offerings and, at the sound of approaching footsteps, he would give out with the plaintive cry of "Pity the poor blind man". It was the first time I had encountered that affliction and my young mind had great difficulty in coming to terms with its implications. Whenever I saw him I unfailingly looked the other way, especially when local urchins played a trick on him by silently moving his enamel mug a few feet away from where he had placed it. Thankfully, there is now no need for blind people to beg in the streets. One has to admit that there are some aspects of life in those "good old days" which we can well do without.

Ted Cook was in a different category, for his main attribute was his basic, uncluttered simplicity. A tall, thin, gangling sort of man, he was always to be seen loping along the streets in his white sand shoes and with a perpetual cigarette dangling from his lips and a basket of fish over his arm, for he was Billy Cox's delivery boy. Local boys took great delight in riding their bicycles close up behind him and furiously ringing their bells in the hope that the shock would cause him to drop his basket. On Saturday nights Ted had another occupation, for it was then that he sold the "Pink Un" outside the Regal Cinema. Crowds of country boys came into Town on those nights and would call out, "How did City get on, Ted?" Ted, however, was not stupid. His answer was always the same: "Buy a paper and find out".

I think the king of all the old Cromer characters must surely have been a man called "Everytime". His real name was John Randall, but nobody ever called him that, although the reason for his quaint nickname remains a mystery. Rumour has it that he was once a successful butcher and that he owned his own cottage just off West Street. At some point, however, he developed an eccentric life-style which led him to live in a wooden shack in the cottage yard, from where he would make daily trips around the town collecting rags and rabbit skins to sell. He also kept a few pigs on a piece of land off the Holt Road and he made himself a kind of wooden box on wheels, in true schoolboy fashion, in which to collect the swill to feed them. His most endearing habit, however, was that of suddenly breaking into a dance in the middle of the road as he went on his rounds. It was a simple affair, first on one foot and then on the other, each accompanied by the chant of "A heel and a toe and a one, two, three". One cannot help thinking that such an activity would put his very life at peril on today's traffic-filled streets.

Hilda Sergent (later Harwood) has good cause to remember "Everytime" for, on one occasion, he happened to call at her home shortly after the family's pet dog had been delivered of a litter of puppies. Her father, seeing this as an opportunity to dispose of one of them, gave one to "Everytime" but, on returning home from school, Hilda was heartbroken to find that he had given away her favourite puppy. She therefore hatched a plot to get it back and, under the cover of darkness, she armed herself with one of the other puppies and, making her way to "Everytime's" shack, carried out a switch. The ploy did not succeed, however, for "Everytime" quickly spotted the difference and was soon back on the doorstep demanding the return of his rightful animal.

"Shrimp" Davies has a further memory which indicates that the man had another side to his character. "Shrimp" was quite a youngster at the time and the traffic was mostly horse-drawn, with only the occasional motor vehicle to disturb the peace. On this occasion, a horse and cart were standing outside a shop and people were quietly going about their business when, spluttering and snarling, a motor car came lunging onto the scene. The sudden noise so alarmed the horse that it took fright and bolted, pulling the cart with it. Disaster appeared to be imminent until a man stepped quietly into the road and, standing in the horse's path, raised his hand rather in the style of a policeman on point duty. The horse, as if controlled by some unseen hand, came to a sudden halt. The man who stood before it was, of course, "Everytime".

"Shrimp" has never forgotten that drama of long ago. "I remember thinking at the time", he said, "What a brave man!" Coming from somebody such as "Shrimp", that is praise indeed.

Football played a big part in the lives of the menfolk of Cromer, and it was to Cabbell Park that most male eyes were turned on Saturday afternoons. There the Town team regularly did battle in the Eastern Counties League against such opponents as Yarmouth, Gorleston and King's Lynn, and it can be said without any suggestion of bias that they were a very talented side. One imagines that there are written records of the men who displayed their skills in those halcyon days but, even in one's memory, the names spring to life as though it was only yesterday.

There was Cecil "Ducky" Swann, a very talented inside forward who, indeed, became a County player, and Reggie Kirby (better known as "Ruchie"), on whom Aston Villa are said to have cast covetous eyes. Quite apart from his footballing achievements, "Ruchie" Kirby had become something of a local hero in a very different field, as we shall hear later. Also among the forwards were such men as Steven Allen, Ernie Griffin and "Winkle" Abbs from Runton, who also had a fine singing voice which he used to great effect with local male voice choirs. The halfback line was full of characters, amongst whom Theo Randall stood out in more ways than one. He has been described to me as "not the best player ever to turn out for Cromer, but certainly the most popular". In his spare time, Theo and his father ran the Band of Hope where, on Tuesday evenings and with the aid of magic lantern shows and little playlets, they sought to warn the younger generation of the dangers of the demon Drink. Physically, they were an ill-assorted pair for, while his father was a small man with white flowing hair and beard, Theo was tall and thin. It was his physique, indeed, which enabled him to score a goal which still lives in the memory of all who saw it. It was during a local derby match against Sheringham and, when the ball came in from the wing, Theo launched himself forward horizontally like a ramrod. He had timed his dive to perfection and the ball cannoned off his head and flew into the net before anybody had a chance to move. In the boyhood parlance of the day, "the goalie never even smelt it". It was the only time Theo ever scored for Cromer and it would be pleasing if one could say that it was the winning goal. The match was not that close, however, and the final result was Cromer 10 Sheringham nil.

Among the other members of the halfback line in those glory days of Cromer football were such men as Frankie Morlett and the brothers Lennie and George Baker, and it was George who figured strongly in another match which still lives in the world of memory. George was a man who put everything he had into every match, and his most renowned asset was the strength of his kick (usually reserved for the ball). It was, indeed, his kicking power which played a vital part in the Norfolk Senior Cup Final of 1921, when Cromer's opponents were Gorleston. The match was played at the Nest, that quaint little home of Norwich City Football Club with its notorious concrete wall running around one corner of the pitch and behind the goal. It was a particularly tough game, so much so that Cromer, because of injuries, were reduced to nine men. Then, with the score standing at 1–1, Cromer were awarded a penalty and the crowd fell silent as George Baker prepared to take the kick. He himself was not in the best of condition, being heavily bandaged around the head, but he strode forward and struck the ball with every ounce of energy he possessed. The ball flew into the goal like a bullet and, stretching the net, struck the concrete wall and rebounded all the way back to the halfway line. It was the goal which brought the Norfolk Senior Cup back to Cromer.

Amongst the wealth of other footballing characters whose names spring to mind are such as Tom Durrant, George Juby, Ivan (or was it Irving?) Gardner and "Taffy" Thompson. "Taffy", however, was not a regular, for he was an engine driver and was not always available. Then, of course, there was "Tuner" Harrison, arguably the greatest gentleman ever to don the colours of Cromer Town F.C. "Tuner" excelled at all ball games, but he is best remembered for his sportsmanship. With "Tuner" it was skill which counted and nobody can recall a single occasion when he deliberately engaged in a foul tackle.

Now, however, we must return to the story of "Ruchie" Kirby and of the day when he became a hero. For this we must go back to

Cromer Footballers of 1922. From left to right; Back row: William P. Baker, Tom "Bussey" Allen, Harry Chadwick, "Tricky" Green, — Todd, Tom Durrant, Sid Leggett, Jimmy Millington, "Daddy" Emms (the local schoolmaster).
Front row: Steven Allen, George Baker, Cecil "Ducky" Swanr, Reggie "Ruchie" Kirby, "Winkle" Abbs, Theo Randall.

the Great War and, in particular, to the ill-fated battle of Gaza which involved the men of the Royal Norfolk Regiment. In those days, the "Norfolks" were a truly county regiment and there could have been few towns and villages which were not represented in its ranks. "Ruchie" Kirby was one of those who found themselves taking part in what was to prove to be the blackest day in the history of the regiment. Indeed, it was to be a day of heartbreak in a multitude of homes throughout Norfolk for, of the 900 men who went into battle, only a mere 40 or so survived. The ill-conceived expedition rapidly became an occasion of mass slaughter, and those few who survived the carnage readily affirmed that the only reason they were able to escape was because of the bravery of their machine-gunner. It was he who had covered their retreat as they desperately struggled to regain the comparative safety of their slit trench, and it was no mean feat, for his was not one of the modern lightweight guns which can be fired from the hip. It was the old-fashioned type of weapon which had to be mounted on a metal tripod and behind which the gunner sat to fire at the advancing enemy.

Several of the men were wounded in the retreat, including a certain Private Blyth who was shot in the leg, but nobody was able to help him. The one man whom they did make a special effort to help was the bombardier, for he had gone into battle with hand grenades strapped round his body. The conflict had been such, however, that he had been unable to use them, and the men feared that, if he received a direct hit, they would all have been blown up with him.

Eventually, the survivors reached their trench and the machine gunner was at last able to join them. It was then that they heard a scraping noise which suggested that somebody was coming over the top. It was Private Blyth with his broken leg. He had strapped his rifle to his leg to serve as a splint and had somehow managed to drag himself to safety. It had been a devastating day for the Royal Norfolk Regiment and a black day in the history of the British Army.

But there were forty men in that trench who, to a man, vowed that they would never have survived the carnage if it had not been for the bravery of their machine gunner. And who, we may ask, was he? Of course, it was none other than "Ruchie" Kirby. Thus it was that the local footballer became a hero and took his place among the list of Cromer's most illustrious sons. After the war, when "Ruchie" came back and resumed his footballing career, visiting teams brought far greater numbers of supporters with them than had been the case in pre-war days. But most of them had not come to see the match — they had come to see "Ruchie".

Cromer men never believed in doing things by halves, and this was as evident on the sporting field as it was in their workaday lives. The football team put everything they had into each match and their enthusiasm was, if anything, more than equalled by that of their supporters. For them, as for the players, every home match became ninety minutes of sweat and toil as they gave vent to their feelings. They must surely have been the most vociferous band of supporters any team ever had, and their cries ranged through every extreme, from hysterical delight at the scoring of a goal to undisguised disgust at what they considered to be an inept performance by the men on the pitch.

Among the men who regularly stood around the touchline was Coxswain Henry Blogg, and the team knew the spot where he unfailingly took up his position. Amongst the wealth of advice which they received from onlookers, it was that which emanated from Henry's direction which fell most upon their ears. It was well known that he would never, under any circumstances, criticise his fellow lifeboatmen, but it was a different matter with football. A piece of clever play might occasionally bring forth some quiet comment such as "Well played, Ducky", but, for the most part, the words which fell upon the players' ears were likely to be critical and somewhat uncomplimentary. Indeed, if Henry had a quiet match, the men knew they were playing well. Yet his remarks were always received without rancour, for he was known to be a great student of the game, as he was, indeed, of cricket.

Henry, himself, never engaged in sporting activities, for he was much too busily engaged in othe matters. But that, as they say, is another story.

Chapter 4
Men of the Sea

The days of my boyhood in Cromer were a time when the mere mention of the name of the place was sufficient to conjure up in most people's minds an image of two things – crabs and lifeboats. The crabs were there first, of course, and they still remain unchallenged as the best to be found anywhere in the kingdom. But the lifeboats, too, have a long history. Ever since 1804 they have been putting to sea, manned by the same men who, in more peaceful times, sought out the crabs from those self-same waters.

As a former coxswain put it to me: "If you're born in Cromer and you fish off Cromer, then you're automatically in the boat. It's not a question of joining – you're born to it". Thus, through the years, the same families have had a succession of men in the lifeboats, and the records are liberally sprinkled with their names – names like Balls, Harrison, Rook, Rix, Cox, Stimpson, Kirby, Nockels and Davies. But, in my childhood days and for long after, there was one name which shone like a beacon across the world and brought fame to the man who bore it and to the town in which he lived. That man was Henry Blogg.

To fully relate the exploits of Henry Blogg would be far beyond the scope of this book. Indeed, it would need almost an entire library to do them full justice and, in any case, his rescues have already been well chronicled. Suffice it to say that, during his 53 years of service with the lifeboats (for 38 of which he was coxswain) he put to sea on no fewer than 387 occasions and played a leading part in the saving of 873 human lives, not to mention that of one dog. He became the most decorated of all lifeboatmen, being rewarded by his country with the George Cross and the British Empire Medal. Three times the R.N.L.I. awarded him its Gold Medal, which ranks alongside the Victoria Cross in status, and four times he received the Silver Medal. And there were many others which came his way, all of which, because of his innate modesty, found their way into a cardboard box which he kept in a cupboard, only to be brought out on rare occasions to be viewed by some privileged visitor.

Millions of people heard of Henry Blogg and many met him, but there were very few who really knew him. Indeed, some of his closest associates have readily admitted how little they really knew about him, for he was an introvert, even a shy man, and he certainly had no great relish for the status of hero which was thrust upon him. I met him many times and spent many hours in his company, but I cannot claim to have known him. Indeed, at that time I was not even aware that he was a hero, for I was very young and to me he was simply my father's friend, which was recommendation enough.

It was at a time when, with my three older brothers at school, my father would sometimes take me out to enable my mother to get on with her work. "Come along", he would say. "Let's go down to the beach and see Mr. Blogg". To me he was always simply "Mr. Blogg" and, as I played on the sand, the two men would engage in deep discussion of matters unknown to me. I liked Mr. Blogg, for he always treated me with the sort of kindness which stemmed from an obvious love of children. And yet there was one aspect of our relationship which bothered me – he gave me the nickname of "Nipper". Now, at that tender age, the only nippers I knew anything about were crabs' claws. When I went to the beach with my mother I would search in the little pools left by the receding tide for the miniature crabs which we always called "kitty witches" and, when I found one, I would hold it up on proud display. Every time I did this, there would come my mother's warning call: "Watch out for its nippers". I just couldn't understand why Mr. Blogg should give me such a name.

My most lasting memory of Henry Blogg, however, is of his eyes and even now, as I look back, it is this aspect of the man which springs most readily to mind. They were soft and gentle and they had a lovable twinkle, but there were other features which almost defy description. There was a great tenderness, but there also seemed to be a hint of sadness, even of loneliness. I have a strong feeling that Henry Blogg was, in fact, two men in one body. One was the hardy hero who risked all to meet the demands of his calling and the other was the tender, loving inner man whose thoughts were only for others. This showed itself in his treatment of his men, for he would never ask them to do what he himself was not prepared to do, and the honours he received were accepted on behalf of "the team" rather than on a personal basis.

That inner humanity was well to the fore when, on that October morning in 1932, he took the *H.F. Bailey* out to the assistance of the Italian vessel *Monte Nevoso*. It was to prove to be a saga of both courage and patience until eventually, after more than forty-eight hours, all the crew were lifted from the stricken vessel. Even then, however, the coxswain refused to leave the wreck until he and some of his men had boarded her to make sure nobody was left on board. It was then that they heard a whimpering sound from the cabin, and, on forcing the door, a large dog crawled pitifully to Henry Blogg's feet. It was a Tyrolean sheepdog, and it was carried to the lifeboat and brought to Cromer with the human survivors.

All members of the crew of the *H.F. Bailey* received medals from the R.N.L.I., but for Henry Blogg there were two other honours. The Italian government awarded him a medal whilst, at home, the Canine Defence League decorated him in similar manner with their highest award. It is difficult to know which of the two gave him greater pleasure, but both of them paled into insignificance six months later when, on release from quarantine, the dog was presented to him. It was his first and only dog (although his daughter later adopted a stray) and he immediately christened it "Monte". The dog soon grew to love his new master and a deep bond developed between them until Monte died in 1935.

Henry Blogg's courage was by no means confined to his sea-going activities, for he had firm views on certain topics and he was never slow to voice them, even in the face of authority. This was never better typified than on the occasion when, with some of his crewmen, he travelled down to the Isle of Wight to take delivery of a new lifeboat. At Cowes, he took his first look at the boat with a marked lack of enthusiasm and, as he took her up the coast, he became steadily more ill at ease. By the time he arrived back in Cromer he could contain himself no longer and, jumping ashore, he made straight for the telephone to inform R.N.L.I. Headquarters that he did not want the boat and would prefer to have the old one back. It was all a question of shape, he explained. She was so narrow and sharp forrard and so big aft, whereas local men liked big bows and smaller sterns. He is reputed to have said that her bows didn't make a big enough hole for her stern to get through. His feelings were very much in keeping with the tradition of East Coast Fishermen that:
> "A cod's head and a mackerel's tail,
> They're the boats to ruddy well sail".

Anyway, Henry made his point and the boat was exchanged for

Henry Blogg and his daughter's adopted stray (Inset: Monte, the Tyrolean Sheepdog he rescued from the *Monte Nevoso*.)

one which met with his approval. There can be no doubt that he did much to govern the shape of local lifeboats, although he never bothered too much about the mechanical side of things. He preferred to leave that to people who understood such matters.

It was not until 1947, at the age of 73, that Henry Blogg decided to retire and give way to a younger man. His was to be a hard act to follow, for he left behind not only an impeccable record of achievement but also a glowing example and inspiration for whoever was to follow in his wake. The new man, however, was well qualified for the task, for it was the old man's nephew, Henry T. Davies, known to everybody as "Shrimp". Not only had he inherited his uncle's Christian name, but his nickname had also come from the same source for, when Uncle Henry had carried out his first inspection of the new family arrival, he had declared, "Well, bless my soul. Tha'ss a little old shrimp you've got there!" The name stuck, and never in all the years I have known him have I heard anybody, not even his wife, call him anything but "Shrimp".

"Shrimp", of course, was born into the lifeboats. "You learnt about it very young", he said. "You would wake up in the night and hear the commotion of father running and mother carrying his boots. They ran just as they had got out of bed, even in their long Johns, and the men would fight for places on the boat". He even recalled one lifeboatman who had been called out on his wedding night.

As the years went by, he sailed with his uncle and, indeed, the two men worked together during the Second World War on some of the most demanding rescues in which the Cromer boats had ever been involved. There was, above all, that fateful morning of August 6th, 1941 when six ships of a British merchant convoy, groping their way down the coast through mist and rain, ran aground on the Sands. It does scant justice to the heroism displayed on that day to merely say that the *H.F. Bailey* rescued 88 men from four of the ships while the No. 2 boat, *Harriott Dixon* and the *Louise Stephens* from Gorleston plucked 31 more from the other two. A total of 119 men had been saved from a watery grave in an action of combined skill and courage which, had it not been wartime, would have filled the front pages of every newspaper in the land.

Then there was the rescue of 44 men from the *English Trader*, grounded on Hammond Knoll in the most appalling weather conditions. There followed many other rescue missions, by which time

44

Henry "Shrimp" Davies.

"Shrimp" had served his apprenticeship and was well prepared for the task which lay before him.

It was not long before his qualities were put to the test for, on July 8th, 1948, he answered a call to the *François Tixier,* a coal ship from Dunkirk, which was sinking after its cargo had shifted. "Shrimp" proved himself equal to the challenge and succeeded in rescuing the sixteen crew members, for which the French authorities gave him the Order of Maritime Merit, the highest award given by that country for lifesaving at sea.

Other honours followed, culminating in the award of the British Empire Medal in 1970, and when he retired in 1976 he found himself appearing on television as the subject of "This is your Life". It has been no ordinary life and now, as he holds court over visiting holidaymakers in his hut down by the beach, "Shrimp" can look back over a wealth of experiences for, whether in war or peace, a lifeboatman never knows when the call may come.

There was, for instance, that day in November 1938 when the people of Cromer suddenly found a war being fought on their doorstep. It was not their own war for, although Europe was in a state of turmoil, it was only a few months since Neville Chamberlain had come back from Munich with his slip of paper and his assurance of "Peace in our time". Indeed, when the first sounds of gunfire echoed over the town, there were those who thought it was merely the army practising at Weybourne Camp. The folk nearer the beach, however, soon became aware that the explosions were coming from out at sea and were the product of a deliberate act of aggression. It was, indeed, an extension of the Spanish Civil War, which had been raging in that unhappy country for the past two years.

We had heard much about that particular conflict, for our newspapers carried daily reports of the civil unrest and resultant carnage which was tearing Spain apart. We knew that the Spanish government, communist by nature and backed by the Russians, was engaged in mortal combat with General Franco's Fascist Insurgents, but it is doubtful whether many of us really understood the full significance of the situation. We had heard about the bombing by the German Air Force of the defenceless little town of Guernica and of the great loss of life which resulted. We had heard about the priests in Spain being killed and we deplored it but, at the same time, it was a long way away. Spain was a much more distant country in those days and there was no television to bring live pictures of the carnage into our living rooms.

The Men of the *H.F. Bailey.*
Left to right: William Henry Davies, Robert Cox, William Thomas Davies, Robert Davies, Jack Davies, Henry T. "Shrimp" Davies, Sidney "Kelly" Harrison, Jack Davies junr., Henry Blogg.

A family of lifeboatmen – "Shrimp" at his Uncle Henry's clifftop memorial with his nephews Richard Davies (now coxswain) and Billy Davies (2nd cox).

I had gleaned a certain amount from my journalistic brother Stanley, who had been out there for some time as a war reporter. Even with such knowledge, however, there was no immediate reason to connect the sudden burst of gunfire off Cromer with that distant conflict. The day had started just like any other, with the people of the district going about their business in the normal manner. Men were at work in the fields, and the ships of the fishing fleet were making their way out to the fishing grounds through calm seas which gave no indication of any impending need to call upon the services of the lifeboat. Henry Blogg, incidentally, was as thankful for that fact as anybody, for he was only just recovering from appendicitis and by no means fully fit.

Out there on those peaceful waters, however, there was one vessel whose crew had reason to view their situation with a certain degree of apprehension. She was the *Cantabria,* a steamship of 5649 tons, belonging to the Spanish government. Having delivered a cargo of Russian timber to the Port of London, she was returning along the Norfolk coast on her way to Leningrad with a human cargo of forty-five people, including women and children. The skipper, Captain Aguelles, was accompanied by his wife and their two young children, a boy of six and their eight-year-old daughter, Veyona.

All had gone well until, in mid-morning, the crew had become suspicious about the actions of another vessel which appeared to be shadowing them. As they viewed her through binoculars, she looked harmless enough but, every time they changed course, she did likewise and, furthermore, she was steadily closing on the *Cantabria.* Then, as the ship came even closer, their worst fears were realised. Looking through his binoculars, Captain Aguelles saw the Insurgent flag suddenly being run up the masthead and, even worse, camouflage being whipped away from the deck to reveal an array of five menacing guns. Their shadow thus revealed herself as being the *Nadir,* an auxiliary cruiser of General Franco's fleet, and there could be no mistaking her intentions when she ran up the international signal "Heave to or I fire".

Captain Aguelles had no intention of giving in to the Insurgents and he continued to maintain a steady course. All the while, however, the gap between the two ships became progressively smaller, and then two shells suddenly hurtled from the guns of the *Nadir* and fell just short of their target. The sound of the gunfire fell upon the ears of not only the folk on shore but also the men of the fishing fleet who were going about their business some distance further out. Incensed by this act of piracy in their waters, they turned as one and positioned themselves between the two Spanish vessels, sounding their sirens and telling the *Nadir* in no uncertain terms (and, no doubt, in the best of Norfolk accents) to take herself off and go elsewhere. At this, the *Nadir* turned away and the fishermen, their task accomplished, took off again to the fishing grounds.

The Spaniards, however, were merely biding their time and, once the fishing boats had gone, they returned to the attack and succeeded in hitting the *Cantabria* with shellfire in several places. At this point, conditions were so threatening that the crew appealed to Captain Aguelles to surrender to the Insurgents, but still he refused. Then, however, the crew of the *Nadir* achieved their main objective by landing a shell right into the *Cantabria's* engine room, thus bringing the ship to a complete halt. For good measure, they went in closer and raked their target with machine gun fire, and it was then that the captain realised the hopelessness of the situation. He, himself, had no intention of surrendering, but he said that those members of the crew who wished to take that action could do so. Accordingly, two boats were lowered. Some of the people on board climbed into one and made for the *Nadir* whilst others filled the second one and went off in the opposite direction, leaving the captain and his wife, their two children and a steward aboard.

At this point, the enemy cruiser at last stopped firing, and then came the sound of an explosion from the shore. This was, of course, the maroons calling out the Cromer lifeboat, the *H.F. Bailey*. Out went Henry Blogg and his men to rescue the five people remaining on the stricken vessel and, though it was not one of their most difficult rescue missions, they were only just in time. Indeed, as they turned towards the shore they looked back and saw the *Cantabria* sink into a watery grave. Meanwhile, the eleven occupants of the other boat were picked up by a steamship, the *Pattersonian,* and taken into Yarmouth.

Needless to say, the events of that day attracted the attention of the world, and all the London newspapers sent their top reporters to cover the story. They, however, had great difficulty in gaining access to the survivors and had to content themselves with official statements. Eventually, as the records show, "an interpreter and a reporter were admitted". The interpreter and reporter were, in fact, one and the same person – my brother. Thus he was able to get the facts of the case for the authorities and also a wonderful exclusive story for the "Eastern Daily Press". A very well-known London journalist of the day attempted to acquire the story by offering my brother a certain sum of money, but anybody who knew Stanley would have known that his loyalty to his paper was such that he would divulge nothing.

Some time after the story had been written, he told me of the way in which Captain Aguelles' little daughter, eight-year-old Veyona, had been unable to control her excitement and continually added her little contribution to the interview.

"Were you frightened?" he asked her.

"I was the oldest of the children, so I just couldn't be afraid", she replied, summoning up all the maturity of her eight years. "The others all wanted to go to the other ship, but I didn't want to go. I wanted to stay with Mummy and Daddy". There she paused for just a second and then declared, "I don't think I want to go to sea again".

The best the London papers could do was, perhaps, best summed up by the one which, in describing the *H.F. Bailey's* rescue mission, declared that "shells were landing in the sea all around the lifeboat". This statement was dismissed by Henry Blogg in his usual forthright manner. I will refrain from quoting his precise words, but he made it clear in his own inimitable style that they hadn't heard a gun fired either going out or coming back.

That, then, is the story of the day when the peace of Cromer was disturbed by the violence of somebody else's war. It caused quite a sensation at the time, yet, within a few short years, it was destined to be overshadowed by the events of another, and vastly greater, war. The next one would not be content to stop just short of Cromer's doorstep and, furthermore, Henry Blogg and his men were destined to be involved in a long sequence of infinitely more dangerous missions than the one which had taken place on that November afternoon.

CHAPTER 5

Regal and Rollerdrome

One of the most significant figures in the life of Cromer in the earlier years of this century was Edward Trollor. At that time he was best known for his fruit and vegetable shop in Church Street, which he himself called "The Cheap Fruit Stores", though most people knew it simply as "Mr. Trollor's". Much of the produce he sold came from the orchards and greenhouses of his own two farms, for he had a hundred acres alongside Hall Road and twice that amount over at Wroxham.

His shop stood cheek by jowl with Austin Beck's central Cycle Stores, and the delightful photograph taken around 1914 conjures up a nostalgic image of the times. In particular, it is the notices on display which paint the picture, with Mr. Beck offering "Bath Chairs, Children's Chairs and Mail Carts For Hire" and, reflecting the impending changes in modes of transport, "Motor Goggles In Stock". Mr. Trollor was offering most fruit at 3d or 4d per pound and bananas at 18 for a shilling, but there is one other sign which is worthy of explanation. Warships of the Royal Navy were a familiar sight off Cromer during the Great War years and occasionally one of them would anchor offshore and despatch a liberty boat bringing crew members into the town. One of the first visits resulted in the purchase from Mr. Trollor of fruit and vegetables for consumption on board the warship. By the following day, his signboard bore the added inscription: "Contractor To The British Admiralty".

For some time before the outbreak of war, Edward Trollor had been considering the possibility of building a cinema on a site in Hans Place which had formerly been occupied by an ironmonger's shop. Eventually his dream became a reality with the opening in June 1914 of what was later to become the Regal, although it did not start life under that name. His policy was to offer a mixed programme of films and stage acts, and thus he called it "Cromer Theatre of Varieties". I feel that the live part of the show must have been somewhat modest in scale, although I have been told that one of the performers who appeared there was none other than Hetty King, one of the foremost Music Hall comediennes of the day.

Edward Trollor's Fruit Stores, c. 1914.

It was a bitter blow when, just two months after the cinema opened, the country was plunged into war and the people of Cromer faced four hard years without the annual influx of holidaymakers. The arrival of troops in the town helped to redress the balance for, though the traders complained that the soldiers' frequent parcels from home meant that they did not spend much money in the shops, at least Mr. Trollor was assured of a regular audience.

It was in the twenties, however, that the cinema began to reach its peak of popularity and it was then that it became our mecca for an evening's entertainment. I suppose the attractions were meagre when compared with today's million-pound epics, for it was the age of silent films and they all came in black and white. Even so, I believe they captivated us more than present-day offerings, for they took us into a world of make-believe. It was the age of imagination rather than the realism which now assails our senses. And, all the while, Edward Trollor ruled over us with an air of unquestioned authority.

It is true that he had a benevolent side to his character, but it is even more true that he was a stern disciplinarian whose rule was law. We knew only too well that any misbehaviour on our part would bring the programme to an abrupt halt. There was even one occasion when my brother was refused admission because he had his popgun with him! Nevertheless, we enjoyed every minute of it and, at the end of the show, we walked out through a thick carpet of orange peel and monkey nut shells.

Mr. Trollor's views on the virtue of hard work were also well known, and they were to bring him into conflict with members of his audience during the General Strike of 1926. William Fulcher and some of his colleagues on the M & G.N. Railway found various ways of whiling away the hours of idleness and, on one occasion, decided to visit the cinema. They were sitting there in peaceful contentment when, with the show about half-way through, the film suddenly stopped, the lights came on and Mr. Trollor appeared. Then, marching down the gangway, he turned to face his audience and said, "It has been brought to my attention that there are strikers present. I will not have strikers in my cinema and they must therefore leave immediately". The little group rose to their feet and made for the exit but, as they did so, William asked whether, in view of the fact that they had only seen half the show, they could have half their money back. "Mr. Trollor's reply", says William, "is unprintable".

The films we watched may have lacked the finesse of today's productions, but the programme lacked nothing in the way of variety. Comedy was a great attraction, with people like Harold Lloyd, Charlie Chaplin and the Keystone Cops well to the fore – and we certainly tended to imitate the actions of our heroes as we went about our daily lives. Jackie Coogan was a special favourite, for he was a young lad of much the same age as ourselves and thus we could readily relate to him. His cap was always several sizes too large and he would wear it with the peak pulled round and hanging over one ear. Any visitor to Cromer suddenly confronted with the sight of hordes of local urchins wearing their caps with the peak hanging over one ear knew straight away that Jackie Coogan was showing at the Regal.

I believe it to be the serials which most captured our imagination, for every episode was cunningly contrived so as to leave our hero or heroine teetering on the verge of disaster. We could hardly wait to get back the following week, and Mr. Trollor was happy, for he knew he had a readymade audience. I suppose the best-known star of the serials was Pearl White, together with her two leading men, Eddy Polo and Elmo Lincoln. Elmo was a tremendously strong man with biceps the size of rugby balls, but I recall one episode which found him in serious danger. By sheer force of numbers, the "baddies" had captured him, pushed him into a hole in the ground and prevented his escape by rolling a massive boulder over the top. Then the picture faded and up on the screen came the usual caption: "DON'T MISS NEXT WEEK'S THRILLING EPISODE". We needed no such exhortation and, the following week, we were rooted to our seats as the picture of that great boulder appeared on the screen. Then, as quick as a flash, the boulder flew skywards and out stepped Elmo, flexing his muscles as though it was all in a day's work. Of course, they had no such things as polystyrene in those days, but perhaps it was papier maché! No such thoughts entered our heads, however, for everything that happened on that screen was true. We knew that to be so, for we had seen it!

Of course, much of the success of the shows was due to the skill of the lady who provided the piano accompaniment. Sitting behind the little curtain which hung from a brass rail, her hands would be poised over the keys and her eyes glued to the screen as she followed every changing mood of the story. "Bells Across the Meadow" and "In A Monastery Garden" would tinkle across to our ears, together with a vast range of improvisations to suit each changing scene. Mrs. Bethel was a mistress of the art, and she was also renowned as a composer. When she retired, Mrs. Cowles took over and continued the high standard which her predecessor had set.

It was then, however, in 1928, that Mr. Trollor installed a pana-trope to provide musical accompaniment for the films. I should, perhaps, explain that a panatrope was an early form of double-headed radiogram with twin turntables. Thus it became possible, by using the gramophone records which were becoming so popular, to add to the show a new dimension which was not possible with a single piano. This innovation, however, was not without its problems. In the first place, the instrument was powered by batteries which needed regular servicing, but this inconvenience was overcome in admirable fashion by George Nash, the Regal's resident engineer. The main difficulty was that it was not possible to switch from one record to another with the speed and precision of those talented lady pianists. Thus, in unskilled hands, there might be times when the musical accompaniment was singularly inappropriate. There could be an exciting chase scene or a stirring battle while the violins were still plaintively rendering "Hearts and Flowers". At the other end of the spectrum, one could have a tender love sequence, or the kind of scene which many of the old melodramas included, where the distraught young maiden was kneeling over the grave of her dead lover and the panatrope was still churning out "Kitten on the Keys" or "Tiger Rag". Having said that, however, I have it on good authority that Mrs. Cowles developed a degree of expertise which ensured that such situations never arose.

It is at this point that I must introduce another name to the story of entertainment in Cromer. We have seen that Edward Trollor now had his shop, his farm and his cinema, but he also had some-thing else which was destined to prove of far greater significance to the history of the town. This was his young son, Norman. It could be said that Norman Trollor was born into the entertainment business, but he was also born into a life of hard work. Almost as soon as he could ride a bicycle, he was acting as delivery boy for the fruit shop and, by the time he was nine years old, he was hard at work on his father's farm. It was at that age, also, that he made his first appearance on the staff of the Regal. Dressed up with smart new jacket and peaked cap, he would stand outside the cinema like some kind of miniature commissionaire. Then he would go inside to make sure that none of the audience switched from the cheaper seats to the more expensive ones and, during the interval, he would go round selling chocolates and sweets.

As the years went by, Norman progressed to other duties which brought with them greater responsibilities. First, he was admitted to the rewinding room, where he would prepare the films for return after they had been shown. Then he became assistant projectionist and, later, chief operator. Another part of his duties involved the return of films after they had been shown, and this called for speedy action to ensure that no extra charge was incurred. I believe that present-day films are hired on some kind of percentage basis but, at that time, there was a fixed charge. Pathé News was 10s 6d, an episode of the serial thirty shillings and the feature film two pounds ten shillings. Thus, it was imperative that, as soon as the show had finished, Norman was on his bicycle pedalling up to the station to get the films on the train back to Norwich. Failure to accomplish this would have incurred more than just the wrath of his father.

At one stage in his career there was a development which was to make Norman's delivery run even more hectic. It was at the time when a Mr. Sadler was running the Casino Cinema at Sheringham and occasionally he found himself without films. A call for help to Edward Trollor resulted in an arrangement by which the two cinemas shared the same films. Thus, the show at the Regal would begin and, as soon as they had got through two reels, Norman would have the job of rushing to Sheringham with them so that Mr. Sadler could start his performance. Then would follow the mad dash back to Cromer for the next reel and the equally frantic return to Sheringham in order that Mr. Sadler would have no break in the programme. Fortunately, Norman had, by this time, graduated to a motor cycle, and he became a familiar sight scooting up and down the coast road on his 1915 belt-driven Douglas. One cannot help wondering what would have happened if he had suffered a breakdown on the way, but it seems that no such calamity ever occurred.

In due course, a great change took place with the arrival of the "talkies". The first of such films to be shown in Cromer, in 1930, was "The Love Parade", which featured Maurice Chevalier and Jeanette Macdonald. This signalled the end of an era in more ways than one, for it was then that Edward Trollor sold the Regal to

Norman, the 9-year-old commissionaire and the teenage film courier.

V.E.H. Cinemas, a Norwich company who were steadily building up a chain of such places. It seems rather sad that Norman was thus deprived of owning the place which had now become his very life, but he continued as manager under the new ownership, and many members of the armed forces, stationed in the area during the Second World War, have cause to remember the entertainment he gave them. Even so, it is probably during the years which followed the war that his cinema activities reached their peak, for it was then that, at his Regal Juniors Club on Saturday mornings, he became a kind of surrogate uncle to something like six hundred children.

In spite of his great success at the Regal, even better things lay ahead for Norman when, in 1947, he became proprietor of the Olympia Gardens in Garden Street. This was one of the oldest places of entertainment in Cromer and, as its name implies, it started its life in the form of an attractive garden. It had a large lawn with a stage at one end, and patrons sat in deckchairs on the grass to enjoy the entertainment. Soon, however, the vagaries of the weather dictated that it should be covered in, and there

The cup-winning Cromer Rovers, with Norman Trollor on the extreme right.

followed a period of entertainment of a sedate nature which reflected the lifestyle of the period. Albert Sandler played his gipsy violin there and Ronald Frankau purveyed his gentle humour. Then, as tastes changed, the Olympia played host to such as Cilla Black, Lulu and the Barron Knights.

By the time Norman Trollor took over, however, youngsters were feeling the need for a more vigorous outlet for their energies. Thus it was that he decided to turn the building into a venue for roller skating, which had been popular in earlier years when the Pier Pavilion had been used for that purpose. Up came the sloping floor and down went a flat one of beech (Norman would have preferred maple, but postwar restrictions made that impossible). It was very much a family affair with Norman and his wife Hilda supported by a group of friends, and it was a family atmosphere which they provided for their patrons.

It was an instant success as crowds flocked there, not only from Cromer and nearby villages, but from many more distant parts of the county. At no time in its long life had the Olympia Gardens known such popularity, and it rapidly became the focal point of the town's entertainment. Many of those who came were renewing the skills they had acquired on the Pier, but many were beginners who were provided with skates and taught how to use them. Furthermore, the tuition was not confined to basic skills, for Norma and Hilda engaged Norfolk's two greatest professionals, Frank Martin and Jocelyne Taylor, to give lessons in roller dancing and figure skating.

The competitive instincts of some of the skaters were also catered for with the introduction of roller hockey and Cromer soon had two teams competing in national competitions. They were known respectively as the Panthers and, rather predictably, the Crabs, although the latter soon changed their name to Cromer Rovers. It was the Rovers who, in 1954, achieved national fame by winning the All-England Cup, beating a team from Herne Bay in the final match at Alexandra Palace by five goals to two. The team on that illustrious occasion comprised Tony and Michael Breed, Norman and Donny Abbs, Freddy Duffield and Norman's son John, who later became a medical practitioner in Australia.

The success of the Olympia Rollerdrome was destined to continue for the better part of thirty years, during which time many romances blossomed among its patrons. A large number of couples met there, got married and, in the fullness of time, took their children along. On Saturdays, many mothers, on their way to do their weekend shopping, would drop their children off there, happy in the knowledge that they would be well looked after.

It is no exaggeration to say that the Rollerdrome became one of Cromer's greatest success stories but, sadly, it was a story which came to an end in 1974. Norman wanted to continue, but his application for a new lease was rejected by the owners, who wanted the building for use as a warehouse. Ten years later came the final ignominy when the building was demolished to make way for a supermarket car park.

It was, above all, Norman Trollor's great love of people which led to his many years of success at both the Regal and the Rollerdrome. When one remembers his many other activities in the town, one can readily understand why he has become one of Cromer's best-loved sons. As one of his former patrons at the Rollerdrome put it to me: "They don't come any better than Norman Henry Trollor".

CHAPTER 6

Those Folk Called "Shannocks".

There dwelt beside the great North Sea
A hale and hearty company
Of men and women brave and free
Who called themselves the "Shannocks".

So began the delightful series of verses written by Miss Bilham and recited with pride by older members of the community at Sheringham Annual Primitive Methodist Bazaar. There, in a dozen simple stanzas, the writer painted her picture of those hardy sea-going men and their equally steadfast womenfolk.

There can be no disputing the fact that the fishermen of both Sheringham and Cromer have always been a rather special breed of men. The nature of their calling demanded qualities not found in ordinary mortals and, though conditions may have improved in recent years, the tradition still survives. Over the generations they led closely-knit lives, both in families and as communities, for the simple reason that they had to work together, to depend upon one another and, above all, to understand each other. It is true that the men now go to sea with motors for their boats and with hydraulic winches, while "her indoors" has a spin dryer and other devices, but life is still far from easy.

What must it have been like, therefore, when, with no radio or other means of communication, the boats used to row and sail out of sight and the men had only the wind, the tides and sheer brute strength to help them? Then, of course, there was their clothing. It was a matter of oiled wool and serge for warmth, long leather boots, and oilskins that really were oiled skin. They allowed for very little freedom of movement and the boots, because they quickly filled with water, were a great handicap if a man went overboard. Many men could not swim, and it has often been said that they would never try to kick their boots off because such action would merely prolong the process of drowning.

The women had to be just as hardy and resolute as the men for, while the boats were away, they were left to shoulder full responsibility for the family — and they had big families in those days.

Sheringham Beach and Promenade.

There were frequently so many children that one can only wonder
where they used to sit. Perhaps it was not too bad at night when
they were all tucked up in bed like sardines, but how on earth did
they manage in those tiny cottages in the daytime? Then, when the
boats came safely back, the cottages would be full of wet ganseys,
slops and oilskins drying by the fire. But the biggest worry for the
fisherman's wife was always "the boat". If it was late home there
was no way of knowing why, and I think that, over the years, the
fishermen and their womenfolk developed some sort of telepathy.
Above all, however, they had a simple faith in their destiny.

There were many occasions, however, when that faith must have
been sorely tested. There was, for instance, the day in February
1916 when Coxswain Obadiah Cooper took the Sheringham
lifeboat *J.C. Madge* to the assistance of the *S.S. Ulla,* in difficulties
off Wells. The weather was as bad as it could have been, with a
strong gale, high seas and a blinding blizzard. Indeed, several oars
were broken before the *Madge* had even cleared the breakers and
then, having located the stricken vessel, there followed the long,
slow haul to get her safely into port at Grimsby. By the time they

reached that haven, the crew had been at sea for forty-eight hours, and the late Jimmy "Paris" West recalled how their frozen clothing had to be slit with a knife to get it off.

They were given accommodation for the night by former Sheringham families who had settled in Grimsby and, in the morning, the men prepared for their return journey. A telegram was dispatched to Sheringham where, having heard no news, the townspeople feared the worst. Indeed, the Vicar was already making a round of visits to console relatives on the loss of their menfolk. The journey home was far less demanding than the outward trip had been for, having been given a rousing send-off by the Salvation Army Band at Grimsby, the *Madge* was towed back by a French vessel and released off the coast at Sheringham. The men then rowed ashore to be greeted with a tumultuous reception, made all the more joyous because, for some reason, the telegram had not been received!

There was one other little incident during that dramatic rescue mission which cannot possibly be omitted, even though it is of little historical significance. Obadiah Cooper was a strict teetotaller and non-smoker and was, indeed, strongly opposed to both vices. Feeling that his men deserved reward for their endeavours as they left Grimsby, however, he made a point of asking if they all had their cigarettes and pipes and tobacco. Yes, they assured him, they all had them. "And", he continued, "have you all got matches?" But not one had as much as a single match. At this, Obadiah reached down by the tiller and produced matches for all the crew. Though he had no use for them, he had foreseen the possible omission and had not wished his men to be deprived of the comfort they derived from a quiet smoke. What a man of great compassion he must have been!

Living so close to death and disaster did not make for moderate shades of opinion and, particularly in Sheringham, the fishermen seemed to be split into two distinct types. Some were wild and unruly characters who spent much of their time, not to mention their hard-earned money, in the local hostelries. They were encouraged in this by fish merchants from out of town who left money at the inns to persuade the fishermen to sell them their catches. Their drinking sessions frequently culminated in street fights which reached such a degree of ferocity that, as one old fishermen put it, "the gutters ran with blood".

In contrast, there were others who held very strong religious beliefs. They had a simple faith in God and a literal belief in the

The *J.C. Madge*, on station from 1904 to 1936.

The *Foresters' Centenary*, which signalled the end of the pull-and-sail lifeboats at Sheringham and served until 1961.

63

Bible, regularly spending long hours searching through its pages for answers to their problems. They were strict observers of the Sabbath and regular attenders at the Methodist chapels, where they endured lengthy sermons of the "hellfire and brimstone" variety, all of which pointed the same moral: "Repent or else". Many of them grew beards which made them look as though they, themselves, had stepped straight out of the pages of the Old Testament.

It was one such fisherman who, having returned from a successful trip, sat studying his Bible and came across a phrase which had an immediate fascination for him. The phrase was "El Nathan" and, on studying the concordance which was always to be found at the back of the old Bibles, he discovered that it meant "God's Gift". Immediately, he and his wife decided that the money he had been paid for his catch had been a gift from God and they would use it to build for themselves a cottage which they would call "El Nathan". They did just that, and the name still survives in Sheringham, although not on the original building. It is now, in fact, the home of Stanley Craske, one of the best-loved of all Shannocks and a veritable mine of information on almost any aspect of life in his beloved Sheringham. I am sorely tempted to refer to him as a local historian and I only refrain from doing so because he, himself, does not like the title. He prefers to regard himself rather as a collector of information and a recorder of memories. Be that as it may, there are many of us who know that, when we enter into that little house in Barford Road, we will be given not only free access to Stanley's accumulated knowledge but also a welcome as warm as any in the kingdom. The name of the house still seems strikingly appropriate.

It was when the men of Sheringham were fishing for herring far away from their native waters that they first came into contact with the Salvation Army, which was well-established at that time in Grimsby. The rousing hymn tunes and, above all, the rumbustuous rhythms of the brass bands had an immediate appeal, particularly for the more shanny characters to whom the inside of a tavern was more familiar than that of a chapel. They took Salvationism to their hearts and brought it back to Sheringham, where they held their first meeting in the old Net Loft on Lifeboat Plain on May 2nd 1888. This was not done without opposition, frequently of a physical nature, for there were those among the local innkeeping fraternity who did not take kindly to the impending loss of income

Early Shannocks.

from men who had previously been their best customers. Salvationism won the day, however, and can now look back over a period of a hundred years during which it has been an integral part of Sheringham's way of life.

Reference was made earlier to the closely-knit nature of the fishing communities of both Sheringham and Cromer, and never did this show itself more forcibly than in times of disaster. It used to be said, with ample justification, that the main cause of death in Sheringham was from drowning, and such an occasion always had a devastating effect on the entire community. Nobody would rest until the body had been found and brought back for burial and, indeed, older fishermen have said that, after such a happening, it was always customary to burn the boat, although I have never heard of this being done in Sheringham. The family spirit which existed right through the community is well illustrated by contemporary reports of such a tragedy in 1893. Daniel and James West were out fishing in a boat which was overturned in a sudden squall and, though James West survived, Daniel was drowned. The local press reported the funeral and described the service at the Methodist Church and then the sad procession of relatives and other fishing families to Upper Sheringham for the interment. It was estimated that about a thousand people attended the funeral and, when one realises that such a figure represented more than half the population of Sheringham at that time, one gets a good idea of how widespread was the sense of loss in the town.

Another glowing example of the community spirit which existed in those earlier days is to be found in the way in which local tradespeople trusted the wives of the fishermen while their husbands were away. The men were gone for quite a long while as they first went to Grimsby and then, following the herring, worked their way down to Yarmouth. During all this while, their womenfolk had no money with which to pay for everyday necessities, but the traders of the town were always prepared to waive settlement until the boats returned. Indeed, this tradition of mutual help sometimes extended even further, for there were often occasions when some boats had such a poor trip that they were unable to meet their commitments. Then, the owners of boats which had been more successful would help their less fortunate colleagues to settle their bills.

Only when this had been done would the members of the crew get together for the "apportionment". This took place at the home of the skipper, where all the money would be put on the table ready for sharing out. Before this could start, however, tradition decreed that a certain proportion of the cash should be set aside and given as a thank-offering to God. A similar practice took place down at Yarmouth, where they called it "Christ's Dole", but at Sheringham it was known as "The Lord's Portion", and it was this money which was used for the building and upkeep of the Methodist Churches in the town.

The next portion of the cash to be taken out was put aside for the maintenance of boats, nets and other equipment and only then would each crew member receive his individual apportionment. But always, in every Methodist fisherman's house, it was the Lord's Portion which came out first.

An early visitor to Sheringham described its inhabitants as being "handsome and insolently independent". I suppose that was what we would now tend to regard as a "back-handed compliment" and certainly one feels that the choice of adverb was more than a little unkind. Independent, however, they have always been, even to the extent of marrying within the parish and jealously guarding their womenfolk from the attentions of outsiders. As Miss Bilham put it:

> "If a strange laddie ventured near
> And smiled upon a maiden fair,
> Who chased that foreigner from here?
> Those jealous lads called Shannocks."

The outcome of this, especially with such large families, was that there was only a limited number of surnames, with each being shared by an increasing number of people. To make matters worse, there was also the traditional handing-down of Christian names, and I am reliably informed that, at one time, there were no fewer than sixteen men named John Henry Grice living in Beeston Road alone. Hence the introduction of nicknames, of which Sheringham boasts a larger number than any other place known to me. Mind you, the Shannocks then complicated the situation by handing down nicknames also in hereditary succession but, though this may prove bewildering to foreigners, they themselves seem to have no problems of identification.

Sheringham nicknames are not only numerous but also wide-ranging in derivation. Some came from certain physical characteristics, as with "Squinter" West, "Spider" Johnson and "Bounce" Craske, but most of them defy the imagination. How, indeed, did "King Kong" and "Butter Balls" Grice get those names or, even more puzzling, those members of the Johnson family known respectively as "Frog", "Maggot", "Snouts" and "Belcher"? Then, what of "Buttons and Bows" Bishop, "Latter-Day" Cox and "Old-Wench" West? The list is endless, with each more puzzling than the last.

One of the saddest periods in the history of fishing off the Norfolk coast was the long years when a state of rivalry, amounting almost to open hostility, existed between the men of Sheringham and their counterparts in Cromer. Nobody seems quite sure how it all started, although each side accused the other of taking up "togs", the small crabs which should be left to conserve breeding stocks. It has been said that they were not above cutting each other's lines at sea, and certainly, when the two towns met in a local football derby, the match usually ended with quite a few "walking wounded", not least among rival supporters who had imbibed too freely. Happily, all that is now forgotten, although it took a tragedy to bring about a reconciliation.

It was in 1931 that three Sheringham men were out whelking when their boat was caught in a storm and they were thrown into the water. The lifeboat *J.C. Madge* was launched but, being of the old pull-and-sail type, she could not reach the men. Appreciating the situation, the *H.F. Bailey* was launched from Cromer with Henry Blogg at the helm and it was this "rival" boat which plucked the men from the water. Two of them, Henry Little and "Sparrow" Hardingham, were little the worse for their ducking, but the third man, Jack Craske, had been struck by the mast when the boat had overturned and was unconscious. Seeing this, "Jack" Davies, the Cromer bowman, jumped into the sea and dragged him to the lifeboat, where "Primo" Allen applied artificial respiration. Henry Blogg then made full speed for Cromer and, in what the Sheringham men later described as one of the most superb feats of seamanship they had ever seen, he held the *H.F. Bailey* in broken surf between the piles of Cromer Pier so that the injured man could be hoisted up onto the deck. Sadly, Jack Craske could not be revived, but it was the action of Coxswain Blogg and his crew that day which finally healed the rift between the men of the two towns. Nowadays there is great mutual friendship, with former rivals fishing together in a way which many thought would never happen.

I think it is inevitable that anybody who lives in daily communion with the sea should, by the very nature of his life, find his activities coloured by superstitious beliefs. This does not only apply to the fishing communities, for their uniformed counterparts in the Royal Navy have many superstitions of their own, but certainly the fishermen of Norfolk seem to have had sufficient to cover almost every facet of their lives. Some stemmed from religious beliefs and others were openly pagan in origin, but the majority were so bizarre as to defy any attempt at rational explanation.

It was religious belief, of course, which decreed that no fishing should be carried out on Sundays. Rarely would any Sheringham boat go out on the Sabbath although, if there was a catch to be had, the men of Cromer did not always show such inhibitions. Similarly, down at Yarmouth when the herring were running, the local men were not averse to a Sunday trip, but the visiting Scottish boats always stayed solidly in harbour. Good Friday, of course, always counted as a Sunday and was treated accordingly. Indeed, any Friday tended to be viewed with suspicion and no fisherman would ever start a new season or use a new boat for the first time on that day.

No talk about animals was ever allowed on board, especially concerning rabbits (which they called cottontails), rats (longtails) and pigs (curlytails). This still survives, although it does not prevent the non-superstitious men from annoying the others by fixing a rabbit skin or similar object to the boat.

Every fisherman carries a shutknife, the handle of which MUST be black. "Shrimp" Davies recalled to me the time in his boyhood when he saw in a shop window a knife with a gleaming white handle and he was determined to possess it. By saving his pennies he was able to buy it and, as he held it in his hand, it immediately became his pride and joy — until his father saw it. Then it was a matter of taking it back and exchanging it for one with a black handle.

It was considered unlucky to go back for anything once you had left your house and, when the lifeboat was called to a launch, it was not unknown for a member of the crew to be seen running to the shed, with his wife padding along behind, carrying his trousers, boots or some other item of clothing which he had forgotten.

One superstition which is difficult to explain concerns the bad luck which women were said to bring with them if they were allowed any sort of contact with a boat. Wives were never allowed on board, although there was a certain degree of latitude when it came to girl friends — the fisherman always seemed able to adapt the superstition when the need arose! Even so, legend has it that "Tuner" Harrison once forgot to put the bung in his boat and, as the pump was unable to cope with all the water which was coming aboard, he had to go ashore at Caister. He always said that it was because his wife had touched the boat that afternoon.

Even worse was the mere sight of a cross-eyed woman, which was sufficient to lead to a fishing trip being called off. The same thing, strangely enough, applied to parsons. As one old seaman put it to me: "If a parson came along when we were getting the boat ready, there wun't be no trip". Similarly, the sight of two nuns walking on the front meant a "3-reef breeze", although I doubt whether such a sight was frequently encountered up at Sheringham.

Finally, there was the belief that the boat should never be loaded from the port, or left hand, side, but that all pots and nets should be put aboard from starboard. This obviously arose from the story of Galilee when the boats came ashore with no catch and Jesus told the fishermen to try again but to cast their net over the other side of the boat. As the Bible tells us, they then caught fish in plenty. I recently had a somewhat amusing experience as an old retired fisherman told me how he had proved this to be true. He had, he told me, taken a parson on a fishing trip and they spent a long time with the line cast from the port side but caught nothing. "Haul in your line, Reverend", said the fisherman and, turning the boat round, told him to cast from the other side. Sure enough, within minutes the parson was catching mackerel as fast as he could pull them in.

"There you are", said the fisherman. "Now you can tell your congregation that the story of Galilee is true, because you've seen it for yourself".

I am sure there must have been a slight smile on my face at this point and I was unable to resist questioning the old man about the superstition of parsons being associated with bad luck.

"Ah, well, yes", said the fisherman. "But tha's a'right if he doon't wear his collar. He's a'right then acourse Davy Jones don't know he's a parson if he han't got on a parson's suit".

Canny folk, these fishermen!

CHAPTER 7
Stewkey Blues and Little Jimmy.

One of the joys of childhood was a day at the coast cockling. There were cockles all the way along the northern shores of Norfolk and, having inherited my father's love of shellfish, there was great pleasure to be derived from both the gathering and the eating of those succulent creatures. They varied slightly in different places along the coast and each village claimed that its own particular variety was the best, but surely there were none to compare with those brought ashore at Stiffkey. The size and the succulence of the "Stewkey Blues" were such as to bring widespread fame to the village which produced them. Huge loads were brought ashore and despatched over vast distances to buyers who eagerly sought "the best cockles in the country".

That being so, it seems slightly ironic that it was Stiffkey's prize product which, in the earlier part of this century, earned for the people of the village a somewhat unenviable reputation. To be more precise, it was the menfolk who were the cause of the trouble, for they took no part in the cockle gathering and stood accused of living on the hard-won earnings of their wives and daughters. Each day, when the tide ebbed, as many as fifty of the womenfolk would leave their male counterparts to their smoking and gossiping and would make their way over the muddy coastal flats. There, with their skirts hoisted up and their bare legs exposed to the biting winds, they would collect their loads of cockles in baskets which became so heavy that they could hardly carry them. But carry them they did, for they were a hardy bunch of Amazons and, furthermore, they brooked no interference from anyone. Indeed, a writer of the period described how he attempted to question the women concerning their strange lifestyle and how he was forced to retreat in confusion when threatened with physical violence. To those sturdy females there was nothing strange about their activities, for they had never known anything different.

Some years ago, in conversation with one of the older male members of the community, I summoned up my courage and

71

Cockle gatherers at Stiffkey.

questioned him about the earlier men of Stiffkey and their unsavoury reputation. His expressionless face gave away no clues.

"Stiffkey", he said, "is where the women wear the trousers – and always have done. We had Women's Lib here long afore anyone else had ever thought of it".

He spoke with such an air of authority that, at first, I was prepared to accept his remarks as statements of fact. But it was his face that gave the game away. It bore the look of benign innocence which so many old countrymen are capable of adopting when they are engaging in some great leg-pull. No doubt a stranger would have been taken in, but I had seen that expression so many times before, and I pursued the matter no further. Perhaps the world will never know the truth about the strange role-reversal of the citizens of Stiffkey.

I felt slightly deflated, for I had wanted to question him about a later event which had brought a degree of notoriety to the village. Indeed, it had not been just an event but, rather, a long-running saga in which the central figure was destined to achieve far greater fame then even the highly-acclaimed Stewkey Blues.

The greater part of my early life was dominated by the world of journalism, for my father gave a lifetime of allegiance to what we always called "The Paper". It was not only the "Eastern Daily Press" which claimed our attentions, however, for my father covered local stories for various national newspapers and he regularly scanned their pages to see how they had dealt with his contributions. His object in doing this was two-fold. Firstly, he would view with disgust the manner in which some sub-editor in London had mutilated the carefully constructed prose which he had submitted. Then, and perhaps more significantly, he would check as to how much of his story had survived that sub-editor's pencil, for he was on a kind of "piecework", being paid one penny per line for such of his work as actually appeared in print.

My father's devotion to his craft will explain why, as a household, we were always surrounded by newspapers. This was a great joy to me, for I was an avid reader from an early age and, when my father had finished with them, I never failed to work my way through every page. That being so, I think it is not difficult to understand my sense of frustration when, in the early months of 1932, all this reading matter suddenly became unavailable to me. My enquiries began to bring from my mother such responses as "Your father hasn't finished with them yet" and similar stalling comments, and it was somehow not even possible to get hold of them even when the news they contained had become stale. It was some considerable time before I discovered that my difficulty arose as a result of a form of blanket censorship imposed by my parents, who considered that some of the contents at that time were unfit for my young eyes. When, very much later, I saw them, I was confronted by such headlines as: "Amazing Charges Against Rector", "Rector's Midnight Call On Waitress" and "Stiffkey's Rector Cheered By His Flock". It was, of course, the scandalous story of the downfall of the North Norfolk clergyman which my parents tried so hard to conceal from me. Little did they realise, however, that every detail was known to me, for my schoolmates and I discussed the case at great length on every day of his trial – and for long after.

I think there is little doubt that the Reverend Harold F. Davidson should never have become a parson in the first place. The trouble was that twenty-seven members of the Davidson family had been in Holy Orders, and his father was determined that he should become the twenty-eighth. He was given a somewhat sheltered upbringing and sent to specially selected schools where it was thought that he would be untouched by the harsher elements of life. This proved to be a mistake, however, for it was while he was attending Whitgift School that he developed a friendship with one of his schoolmates, Leon Quartermaine, who was destined to achieve fame as a Shakespearean actor. The young Harold Davidson found that he, too, had not only a talent in that direction but also a distinct liking for the Bohemian lifestyle which, at that time, went with it. In spite of his lack of physical presence (he stood only 5ft 3ins) he achieved a fair degree of success, being particularly acclaimed for his portrayal of the leading role in "Charley's Aunt".

His academic progress inevitably suffered and it was only because of help from influential friends that he was accepted at Exeter College, Oxford. Even then, it took him five years instead of the usual three to obtain his Bachelor's degree, for he could never resist the temptation to accept any theatrical engagement which came along. By then, he had developed into something like a combination of two different people. On the one hand there was the showman who was to dominate his life right through until his tragic last days. On the other there was the saviour of young girls, a mantle he had adopted one foggy night when he had saved a country girl, penniless and without friends, as she attempted to end it all in the murky waters of the Thames. This was destined to be his mission in life, and no doubt all would have been well if only he had stayed in London.

In May 1906, however, fate decreed that he should be presented to the living of Stiffkey, that tiny Norfolk village which hitherto had been known only for those delicious cockles. He took with him his new bride, and the villagers, welcoming him with an affection which never waned, immediately christened him "Little Jimmy". What should have been a life of bliss, however, quickly turned to a torrent of continual bickering, and Little Jimmy soon began to seek solace in his beloved Soho with the young girls whom he strived to save from prostitution and degradation. As soon as the Sunday services were over, he would discard his clerical collar and be on board the first available train for London. There he would spend the next six days, only arriving back in Stiffkey in time to don his surplice for the Sunday morning service. Indeed, the lady organist of the time was quoted as saying that she frequently had to keep playing voluntaries "to keep the congregation from growing restless".

REV. H. DAVIDSON M. A.
WELL KNOWN AS THE RECTOR OF STIFFKEY.
PHOTOGRAPHED AT THE FAMOUS BARREL EXHIBITION BLACKPOOL 1933.

There can be no doubt that Little Jimmy did much good work on his visits to London, particularly with regard to the Dockland Settlement, a charitable organisation formed to aid under-privileged boys in the East End. It was the young girls who were his main interest, however, and it was not unknown for him to bring one or two home with him and expect his wife to give them employment about the house. It would seem that, at such times, he was courting disaster, for she was a domineering woman and did not share the almost saintly opinion of him held by the remainder of his Stiffkey flock. Relations between them became greatly strained until relief came in the form of service in the Royal Navy in the 1914–18 War. When, on his return after demobilisation, he found his wife expecting a child of which he was not the father, the marriage was at an end, although they never separated. He threw himself even more vigorously into his work in Soho, and it was said that the only occasion on which he ever spent seven consecutive days in his parish was during the General Strike in 1926, and that was simply because the trains were not running.

Sadly, Davidson was no diplomat and it caused him no concern if he ruffled a few feathers here and there as he went about his task of rescuing young female souls. Unfortunately for him, some of the feathers he ruffled were those of Major Philip Hamond, church-warden at Morston, magistrate on the Holt bench and in all ways a pillar of local society. As a 19-year-old in the Boer War, Major Hamond had become the youngest holder of the D.S.O. in the British Army and he followed this in the Great War with the M.C. and a bar to his D.S.O. As a military man, he had firm views on discipline, and his first complaint about Davidson concerned his slackness in parish matters. Then, when he heard that the young ladies who were frequent guests at the Rectory were going out at night and disporting themselves with some of the local menfolk, his anger knew no bounds. Thus it was that Dr. Pollock, the Lord Bishop of Norwich, received a formal complaint against Davidson under Article 2 of the Clergy Discipline Act.

The Bishop was very much a man of peace and his great wish was to avoid a public scandal, but it was not to be. Private detectives were hired to shadow the Rector and to find witnesses who would be willing to testify against him. Fleet Street editors began drooling over their desks in anticipation of the wealth of salacious material which would shortly fall into their laps. Dr. Pollock would probably have welcomed an informal chat with the Rector,

A postcard issued by the Rector's supporters.

followed by a quiet resignation which would enable the whole affair to be swept under the episcopal carpet. Little Jimmy, however, brought his showmanship to the fore, even to the extent of proclaiming his intention of calling upon no fewer than 481 witnesses in his defence.

The trial opened on March 29th, 1932 and, as day succeeded day, the whole affair became steadily more and more sordid. As the accusations against Davidson steadily increased in both number and seriousness, so his supporters counter-attacked with allegations that prosecution witnesses had been bribed with everything from cash to port wine (one girl was quoted as saying, "I forget what happened after the seventh glass"). The entire proceedings reflected credit on nobody involved in the unpleasant affair, and it must have come as a relief to most (except, perhaps, the editors of certain newspapers) when, on July 8th, the trial finally ended.

Little Jimmy was declared to be guilty of "systematically misbehaving himself with young women" and, as a final thrust, was ordered to pay the costs. This was a gesture of supreme optimism, for the little man was already in a state of bankruptcy. Thus, the

77

Church Commissioners found themselves faced with a bill for £8,205 (which, incidentally, was four times the cost of bringing Crippen to trial). Although the decision concerning his guilt was reached on July 8th, it was not until October 21st, at a ceremony in Norwich Cathedral, that the Reverend Harold Davidson was "removed, deposed and degraded". The Bishop explained that he had left a period of three and a half months in case of a possible appeal, but it has always struck me as somewhat lacking in good taste that, in a parish so close to the birthplace of Lord Nelson, the final ignominy should have been delivered on Trafalgar Day.

Little Jimmy had reached the age of 57 and was destined to live the remainder of his life in a state of penury, but he never lost faith in himself or in the rightness of his cause. He had many supporters who believed that he had been treated unjustly and, in Stiffkey itself, it has always been impossible to find a single person who would say one word against him. In London he was greeted by a thousand people and took five curtain calls when he returned to the stage as a variety act at the Prince's Cinema in Wimbledon. "I am doing this", he said, "because it is a question of either sponging on my friends or of using what gifts God has given me". Gradually, his public appearances became more bizarre and, before long, he became a kind of fairground exhibit, sitting in a barrel on the promenade at Blackpool and proclaiming his innocence to the holidaymakers who paid twopence a time for the chance to look at him. Various other appearances of a similar nature followed until, in 1937, he accepted the challenge which was to lead to his final downfall. This took him to Skegness Amusement Park, where he played the part of a modern Daniel, sharing a cage with two lions. It was there that, on July 28th, he was mauled by one of the lions, receiving injuries of such severity that he died just two days later.

His life ended in the local Cottage Hospital, but the legend and the mystery of the man was destined to live on. Was he really such a rogue as the Church had claimed? A fool, certainly, but surely not a villain. No saint, perhaps, but surely more sinned against than sinner. A ruffler of feathers, indeed, and perhaps it was that which really caused his downfall. It was said that he was more trouble to Bishop Pollock than all the other 900 clergymen in the diocese. The twin roles of showman and saviour of young girls were probably not the best attributes for the incumbent of a rural Norfolk parish. How different it might have been if Little Jimmy had been content to settle for "Charley's Aunt".

CHAPTER 8

Old North Walsham.

I first became acquainted with North Walsham in the mid-twenties, a period when there was still much poverty and deprivation although, strangely enough, there always seemed to be an air of contentment about the place. Our lifestyle was simple in nature and seemingly never-changing, although there had been much change in the previous thirty years or so, as I have discovered when talking to older members of the community whose memories go back to the turn of the century.

One of these is Arthur Whitwood who, when I first met him, was approaching his ninetieth birthday. In his boyhood, none of the roads, not even the Market Place, was surfaced and in dry weather the dust and grit blew around with gay abandon. It became even worse when coal was delivered, for most of the shops had coal holes out in the road, down which supplies were tipped. This must have been distinctly unpleasant for the people who lived in those basement areas, but help was usually at hand in the form of Mr. Rolfe, who lived at Spa Common and drove around with the water cart.

At that time, the town drainage system consisted merely of open channels which carried waste along by the sides of the roads. These ran down towards Mundesley Road where, connecting with a simple sewer, their contents went on their way down Gas Works Loke into the small stream known as the Town Drain, and thence into the river at Swafield. Because of the dusty state of the roads, the drainage channels frequently had a tendency to become blocked, and it was then that "Bruff" Hewitt and Dan Mount set about the task of rectifying the situation. "Bruff" and Dan were the Town's roadmen, and their duties included collecting water in a large wheelbarrow from the Town Pump in the Market Place and flushing the channels clear. It was this pump, a large cast iron construction surmounted by a gas lamp, which provided a large part of the town with its water supply and, although some householders had their own wells, there were many others for whom the daily trek to the Market Place was a necessity of life.

"Bruff" Hewitt and Dan Mount at the Town Pump in North Walsham Market Place.

Dan Mount flushing out the drainage channels.

Lighting at the turn of the century was also somewhat basic, most householders having to content themselves with the light of paraffin lamps. A few were able to boast of a gas supply but, until the arrival of mantles, the light came merely from open jets. It was the same basic system with the street lighting and, for this, the lamplighter would set out at dusk with his long pole to light the jets. Then, at 11 p.m., he would return in order to put them out again. In today's brightly-lit society, that may sound a strange practice but, in those earlier days, most people were in bed long before that time, for little work could be done after dark and they found it more appropriate to be early risers. Almost everything was on the move by 6 o'clock in the morning, for that was when most farm workers started their day, and even the shops were open by eight o'clock.

Under normal circumstances, the only person who was active during the hours of darkness was the driver of that most essential of all vehicles, the nightcart. In some places this conveyance was given the title of "honeycart", and I am reliably informed that the one down at Long Stratton had a bell and was known as the "humdinger". We, however, referred to ours as the "covered wagon" because of its marked resemblance to those horse-drawn vehicles portrayed in so many of the cowboy films with which Mr. Coates entertained us in the Picturedrome.

Two names spring readily to mind as drivers of the covered wagon. One was Sam Howard and the other, who, for reasons which will shortly become apparent, figures most strongly in people's memories, was Billy Blazer. Billy had the reputation of being partial to a drop or two of alcoholic beverage before starting his round (who could blame him?) and sometimes his over-indulgence led to his being somewhat unsteady on his feet. In later years, it was the householder's responsibility to bring the lavatory pan from its normal place of use and to put it outside the front door of the house in readiness for the collection of its contents. In those earlier times, however, it was customary for the nightcart man to go down to the bottom of the garden to get it and then, after emptying it, to return it to its appointed place. Unfortunately, some of the houses had no back way so, when the occupants went to bed, they had to leave the front door unlocked and Billy would go through the house and down the garden to collect the pan. Sadly, there were times when Billy, being slightly unsteady in his gait, failed to get the complete load through the house, which is why his name still lingers in the memory of many people. The aroma which assailed the nostrils of the unfortunate sufferers when they awoke on the following morning was not always conducive to the eating of a hearty breakfast.

Furthermore, Billy tended to carry evidence of his calling with him, even when off duty, and I have been told by a lady whose parents kept a tobacconist's shop that they always found it necessary to leave the shop door open for a couple of hours after he had been in to buy his Woodbines. On one occasion the tobacconist tried, as diplomatically as possible, to get the message across to Billy that his presence in the shop was causing some of his customers to take their business elsewhere, with a consequent loss of income. Billy, however, was unrepentant.

"I don't know what you're prattling on about," he said. "If you had as many customers as I've got, you'd have something to grumble about".

Another essential vehicle of the day was, of course, the fire engine. I well remember the motorised model, with solid tyres and built, I believe, on the chassis of a Model T Ford. Prior to that, however, the vehicle was horse-drawn, with the horses being supplied by Archie Burrell who ran a carrier's business in Bacton Road and made regular weekly runs to Norwich. When one remembers that there were no telephones in those days one begins to wonder how successful those early firefighters were in saving burning buildings, particularly those with thatched roofs. Indeed, Arthur Whitwood has a memory, as a small boy, of seeing a man riding frantically into Town on a horse, which was foaming at the mouth, to tell them to set off the maroons because there was a fire at Edingthorpe. They then had to go and catch the horse and, if the fire was right in the village of Edingthorpe, it must have been at least three miles from the Fire Station. One cannot help thinking that the fire was going quite nicely by the time they got there.

For most of my father's period in office as the local representative of the Press, he never enjoyed the luxury of a telephone. Thus, on the outbreak of a fire, he knew no more about its location than any other member of the community. We would all count the number of rockets which were sent up, for two indicated that the conflagration was within the area of the Town, whilst three meant that it was somewhere out in the countryside. Without further knowledge, however, my father could do no more than await the return of the fire brigade and obtain details from them.

When he was eventually supplied with a telephone, however, the situation was greatly improved, for the firemen were able to give him a call just before they set out and it was then possible for him to get to the scene of the outbreak and produce an eye-witness account. He did not, of course, travel on the fire engine but, instead, followed behind on the sturdy old bicycle on which he daily covered vast distances in that area of North Norfolk. Thus, he would set off past the terrace of houses in which we lived, across the Market Place and then away into whichever part of the countryside his story was to be found.

It was not long before the local lads became aware of this and, as soon as the first rocket went up, they would get on their bicycles and make for the corner of the Market Place to await his emergence from the Terrace. Then, as he set off for the scene of the outbreak, he would be followed by a little posse of young cyclists, looking for all the world like some two-wheeled Pied Piper. Bob Farman, of the renowned thatching family, recalls one occasion when they followed him all the way to Ridlington.

The Captain of the Fire Brigade, Albert Walker, was a well-known figure in the town for, quite apart from his business as proprietor of a cycle shop, he was Chairman of the Managers of the Council School and, in his spare time, a ventriloquist and conjurer. He used two dummies in his act, a man and a woman, one of which he held upon each knee, and he became highly acclaimed as "Professor Walker and his Talking Dolls". He was also no mean performer as a conjurer and was always greatly in demand at functions of all kinds. Ben Scott, now in his nineties after a lifetime as a wherryman on board the *Bertha*, recalled for me the occasion when, as a very small boy, he was conscripted into service as Captain Walker's assistant.

It was at a time when Friendly Societies such as the Foresters and Oddfellows played a big part in the lives of the working people, for there was no Welfare State and the "Clubs" were there to provide something to fall back on when times were hard. Ben's father belonged to the Oddfellows, and it was at their annual Club Feast at the Church Rooms that, after the meal, Professor Walker picked little Ben from the audience and told him to borrow a gentleman's watch and chain for the next trick. The little boy did as he was told and then stood by as the watch was put inside a tin, which was then covered with a cloth. Then, to Ben's horror, Professor Walker proceeded to flatten the tin with a hammer. The poor little chap almost collapsed up there on the stage, for he somehow felt responsible for that precious timepiece. Then, however, Professor Walker removed the cloth and revealed the tin – completely intact. That was by no means the finish, however, for, when the lid was removed, the tin was found to contain a collection of little toys which the conjurer proceeded to distribute among the younger members of his audience. And the watch was returned intact to its owner.

The friendly societies and clubs were a vital feature of life in those earlier years of the century, for they were often the only way in which the poorer members of society could avoid going on Parish Relief or, indeed, into the workhouse. Thus, they were well supported, particularly on Demonstration Sunday. This was the day when all the societies, adorned with their regalia and accompanied by bands, gathered in the Market Place and paraded round the town to collect funds. The main driving force in the Ancient Order of Foresters at that time was Brother Wesby, and he would be at the head of the procession, dressed in his forester's costume and carrying a long pole with two bags at the top. This he would hold up to the windows above the shops to receive offerings, for many people lived above their businesses. When I first heard about Demonstration Sunday, I was told that the Unions also took part, and I thought it strange that trade unions should raise funds in that manner. I was mistaken, however, for the unions involved were, in fact, the groups of parishes which, under the Poor Law Act, were made responsible for the welfare of their paupers. The parish relief in North Walsham at that time was administered by Mr. Hewitt and, every Thursday, the poor and destitute would line up outside a little building in Ship Yard, where they would receive their weekly hand-out of about 3s 6d. This, it should be remembered, was at a time when farm wages were thirteen shillings per week.

When those wages were increased to fifteen shillings, the farmers protested that they could not afford to pay such a large increase. An elderly retired land worker told me of the reaction of his particular boss. He and his colleagues were sitting in a turnip shed eating their breakfast when the farmer entered and proceeded to make it plain that, if they were to have such a big increase in their pay, he would expect it to be reflected in increased output on their part. This was too much for one of the men, who daringly made the suggestion that, in his opinion, a mere two shillings was not much of an increase.

Brother Wesby of the Foresters.

"I don't know about that", replied the farmer. "I don't think you do too bad. You've all got Sunday suits and you've all got bicycles. And another thing – I can't afford to eat cheese like you are there".

At this, the man took his knife and drew it across his lump of cheese. Then, sticking the knife into it, he held it up, saying, "Here you are, master. Have a bit of my cheese". But it was not cheese that the master took from the knife – it was boiled swede.

In spite of the austerity of the times in which they lived, the people of Britain were never slow to seize the opportunity of celebrating a royal occasion, and the folk of North Walsham were always to the fore. Queen Victoria's Diamond Jubilee in 1887 was marked by a celebratory meal, but that, of course, is now beyond living memory. Not so the Coronation of King Edward VII in 1901, however, for this was something else which figured in the remarkable memory of Arthur Whitwood. It was an open-air tea party for the children on that occasion, and Arthur remembers sitting at a table in the Market Place "right opposite where Boot's Chemist's Shop now is". Young Arthur was barely three years old and he remembers his mother standing by him throughout the meal. "And", he told me, "I can remember the boy who sat next to me – he ate so much he was sick". He paused for a second and then added, "But it didn't seem to do him much harm – he only died just a few months ago". I asked Arthur if the children were given Coronation mugs to celebrate the occasion. "No such luck", he replied. "But we ate our tea from cardboard plates with a photo of King Edward in the bottom, and we were allowed to keep them".

When it came to the Coronation of King George V and Queen Mary on June 22nd 1911, the authorities obviously decided that it should be a day which nobody would forget, for no less than 3,100 people sat down at 57 tables in the Market Place for a meal which could hardly be described as a light snack. Arthur described it to me as "a good dinner, with roast beef and all the do's". Official records give rather more detail and tell us that the meal "included 213 stone of beef and 78 stone of puddings made to the recipe used for the Queen Victoria Diamond Jubilee". One cannot think that many fast times were recorded at the children's sports which followed.

It was undoubtedly a great occasion but it seems, perhaps, slightly ironic that it should have come just at a time when the Church authorities were running a soup kitchen for the poor of the parish. The district visitors called on the needy and gave them

North Walsham Coronation Party June 22nd, 1911.

tickets which they could then present at the Old Vicarage in exchange for a free bowl of soup. Local schoolchildren, many of whom walked a long way to school from surrounding villages, were also allowed to avail themselves of this facility, although they were required to pay a ha'penny a pint for the privilege.

Life in those early years of the century was, of course, still largely governed by the strict tenets of Victorianism and there were few who would dare to flout the conventions of the day. It was very much a class-conscious age in which everybody was expected to know his place. Boys were taught to touch their caps to their elders and betters, and girls to be ladylike at all times.

Sunday had been, above all, a day of conformity, particularly with regard to Church and Sunday School. The gentry had always attended morning service, the men in their frock coats and top hats and carrying walking sticks, and the ladies with their massive hats and parasols and long dresses which trailed on the ground if they were not held up. Then there was the traditional Sunday afternoon walk to such places as Captain's Pond, by the side of the main road at Westwick. So popular was this spot, indeed, that it used to be said that walkers needed to make an early start if they wished to find a seat on the post and rail fence which separated it from the road. Present-day traffic conditions, with motor cars rounding the bend and speeding down the hill past the lake, would now make such a simple pastime a hazardous activity. Even in earlier days it was not without its dangers, for it was there that William Cooper, the renowned North Walsham coachman, lost his life when he succeeded in overturning the "Pilot" coach.

For most people Sunday was the day of rest. The children could read and go to Sunday School, but playing games was very much frowned upon. They were not even allowed to cut their nails on a Sunday lest the Devil should haunt them through the coming week. There were many aspects of Victorianism which we can well do without, but there were others to be cherished for, irrespective of one's religious beliefs, Sunday was the anchor day for the family. And it was family unity which stood at the very core of the social structure.

When I first set foot in North Walsham there were already marked signs of an escape from Victorianism, but it was still the family which was the dominating factor in our lives.

CHAPTER 9

Country Characters.

One great feature of my boyhood was the wealth of characters who abounded in the countryside. I suppose there may well be similar people today, although they would most likely be classed simply as eccentrics. In those earlier days many of them were regarded as simpletons or, in some cases, village idiots, although that phrase was never used with any degree of malice. I suppose the main cause of their existence was the lack of educational facilities which resulted in most of them being unable to cope with anything more than the basic necessities of life. Almost without exception they had a simple charm, and one cannot help feeling that our life would have been the poorer without them.

One of the most renowned of those early characters was a man whose name has long slipped from my memory but who used to stand, rope in hand, outside the Eel's Foot Public House at Ormesby throughout the hours of opening time. It was the age of horse-drawn transport and, as each customer drove up with his pony and trap, he would step forward and, with a touch of the forelock, say, "Hold your horse, master?" He was well known to most of the patrons of the hostelry and, rather as a gesture of pity, they would accept his offer and, on their return, would reward him with a sixpenny piece. For many years he did rather well out of this practice, but then came the period when the popularity of the horse began to wane and the motor car began to take its place. He was not deterred, however, and he continued to stay at his post. Then, as each spanking new motor car pulled up, he stepped forward with the same request, "Hold your horse, master?" The motorists, taking pity on the poor old fool, allowed him to tie his length of rope to some part of the car and stand there holding it while they sought refreshment within. But he was not such a fool, for he still earned his sixpences.

Nearer to our own territory, at Banningham, lived Herbert Ribbons, a land worker who, far from being an idiot, was a man of endearing simplicity. I think his education had been basic in the extreme, and he lived his life within the limits of his intelligence. If he bought something and the change came to three halfpence, he insisted on receiving three halfpennies. It was no good offering him a penny and a halfpenny – if he didn't get three coins he was sure he was being swindled. There was also an occasion when he bought a cockerel from his boss who, on being asked the price, replied, "Well, do you think a crown would be about right?"

"Oh, I don't know about that, master", said Herbert. "I was thinking more like five shillings".

When he had first started work for that particular farmer he had, quite naturally, been anxious to know what wages he would receive, but the farmer had been quick to allay his fears.

"Don't you worry about that", he said. "I'll pay you what you're worth".

Herbert's face fell. "Thass no good to me, master", he said. "I'm getting more than that already".

Herbert's boss was, in fact, one of the better ones as regards the manner in which he looked after his workers. Every year he treated them to a dinner at Aylsham "Dog", and it was at one of these annual functions that Herbert caused a certain degree of mirth amongst his workmates. Most of the men either walked or rode bicycles, but Herbert had a small pony, with an equally small cart, in which he did all his travelling. On the night in question, the men assembled at the "Dog" but, at the appointed hour for the meal, Herbert had not arrived. Tankards were refilled and it was decided to wait a bit longer but, as half an hour went by and there was still no sign of him, the boss decreed that the meal should start. It was just as the men were sitting down around the table that the sound of carriage wheels on the gravel outside announced the arrival of Herbert with his little pony and cart. But, as they looked through the window, the sight which greeted them was one which made the entire assembly fall about with laughter, for the little pony was standing forlornly in the body of the cart and Herbert was between the shafts, dejectedly pulling his vehicle up to the door. It transpired that, halfway between Banningham and Aylsham, the little pony had "gone weak at the knees" and Herbert had decided upon the role-reversal as the best way of completing the journey.

The incident had a sequel a week or two later when Herbert decided to sell the pony at Ireland's Sale in Norwich. At the same Sale, with the money he received, he bought a new pony, but he unfortunately omitted to check its measurements. Thus, when he went to instal it between the shafts of his little cart, he soon discovered the awful truth – it was too big. He made the journey back to Banningham as passenger in a friend's vehicle, with the new pony and the little cart trundling along behind. Then came the discovery that the stable was not big enough, but Herbert was not deterred. It was simply another of life's little problems, and he just set to work and built a bigger one.

The countryside was liberally sprinkled with tramps and vagrants who trudged the lanes from village to village and slept wherever shelter could be found. They were mostly out-and-out beggars and we, as children, found them somewhat frightening figures. One wanderer who came into a different category, however, was Louisa Pestell, affectionately known to all simply as "Lou".

Lou came from a good family backgound and it was her own choice that she should forsake the comforts of home for the open road. Nobody is quite certain why she came to that decision, but it is generally believed to have resulted from a broken romance while she was working at Trunch in her younger days. Her wanderings took her over a wide area of north-east Norfolk, stretching from North Walsham up as far as Northrepps, through Trunch and Ridlington to Stalham and back to the North Walsham area, not forgetting the dozens of villages in between. Dressed all in black, with her long skirts hiding her feet, she wore a shawl over her head and carried her belongings either in a sack slung over her shoulder or sometimes in a kind of wicker basket. Everywhere she went she became a familiar and much-loved figure, and the emotion which transcends all others in the minds of those who still remember her is one of compassion, almost of love.

Obviously well-educated, she was quiet in her speech, with a marked tendency towards quoting from the Bible. Perhaps it was her religious leanings which influenced her choice of sleeping quarters for, while it was the custom for barns and outbuildings to be left unlocked for her whenever she was known to be in the area, she seems to have had a marked preference for chuch porches. A lady whose mother used to clean the little church of Beeston St. Lawrence recalls that it was quite a regular thing to find her asleep on the stone floor of the porch at 5 o'clock on a Sunday morning. "She would waken at our approach", she told me, "and with a polite 'Good Morning' would put on her hobnailed boots and move

Lou Pestell.

93

off." She made the same choice at Bradfield and also at Lessingham, where the verger often came across her lying in the porch and would tread quietly past so as not to disturb her.

Lou was never known to beg for either money or food, but many a householder answered a knock at the door to be greeted with a request for water to make a cup of tea. At Lessingham, however, it went slightly further, for there it was the custom for her to present herself at the verger's cottage with apples that somebody else had given her. These the verger's wife would turn into delicious apple dumplings, with lavish helpings of brown sugar. Even then, however, she resisted all attempts to persuade her to go inside the cottage to eat them, preferring instead to take her meal on the little wooden bench outside the back door. Then, with a polite word of thanks, she would go on her way.

Although the story of Lou Pestell is tinged with sadness, it was not without its lighter moments. In particular, there was the very dark night, with heavy black clouds and no moon, when she settled down in the porch of Bradfield Church. At the same time, a poacher was going about his business in the nearby woods until, almost without warning, the heavens opened up and torrential rain began to fall. Looking for shelter, the poacher hurriedly made for the church porch where he sat down to await the end of the storm. Because of the darkness and the fact that Lou was dressed in black, he was completely unaware of her presence until, suddenly, a hand came up out of the darkness and tapped him on the shoulder and a voice said, "What's the time, mister?" The poacher lept up in panic and, dashing through the rain, made for the safety of his home, where he vowed that never again would he set foot in Bradfield Church.

Lou led the life of her choosing for many years until, in 1933, she became ill and was taken to Aylsham Infirmary, where she died at the age of 76. There may be those who deplore the fact that she was allowed to engage in her particular kind of life, but anybody who knew Lou would have been well aware that, for her, a life between four walls would have been like a prison sentence. As it was, she was allowed to lead her life in the way she wanted, without interference from anybody. And who could want for more?

Much of the contentment of our early lives stemmed from the fact that, having seen none of the developments which have more recently taken place, our aspirations were limited to what we knew to be attainable. There were, indeed, no wild parties on New Year's Eve, for we knew that there was little likelihood of the next year being very much different from the one which had preceded it. This is not to say that the odd glass was not raised in hope on that occasion or, indeed, at many other times during the year. In fact, the excessive consumption of alcohol by some members of the community was viewed with such concern that the youngsters, from a very early age, were subjected to a steady barrage of sermons concerning the evils of the Demon Drink. The Band of Hope, at its meetings in the big room above Mr. Willey's bicycle shop, encouraged its members to "sign the pledge" almost before they knew what it was all about, and the School Log of the period carries frequent entries to the effect that: "The children were given the afternoon off to attend the Temperance Festival".

I have little direct knowledge of the extent of the drink problem, but there can be little doubt that it was the womenfolk who suffered most. They were hard times for many families and, while a man who felt so inclined could pop into a public house to drown his sorrows, such action was not acceptable for a woman. Women had yet to be "liberated" and, apart from the few who might call at the side door with a jug, they mostly had to stay at home and attend to the needs of the large families with which the lack of birth control had burdened them. Indeed, perhaps the saddest aspect was the fact that the money being spent on drink could have been put to much better use in the housewife's purse.

One great contrast which springs to mind is that over-indulgence in those days never seemed to lead to the gratuitous violence and vandalism which now seems so prevalent. There were times, on Saturday nights and on festive occasions, when a few revellers could be seen around the Market Place, but they tended to be regarded as figures of ridicule as they made their noisy way home. Most men who imbibed too freely, however, seemed merely to want to go to sleep. After a long Sunday morning in the hostelry of their choice, closing time at 2 o'clock would be followed by an afternoon in bed. It was said, in fact, that the reason why North Walsham children were so well-behaved was that most of them were conceived on a Sunday. One can, perhaps, be forgiven for thinking that this was by no means unique to North Walsham.

With so few motor cars on the roads there was little cause for concern about the combination of drinking and driving. Indeed, there were times when, having reached the stage of somnambulism which resulted from over-imbibing, it was a distinct asset to have a vehicle available, preferably of the one-horse-power variety. In choosing to tell the story of Jack Hall I have no wish to suggest that he was by any means in the habit of drinking himself into a state of intoxication. Indeed, he became one of the best-loved and most highly respected tradesmen of the town as he carried on his florist's and fruiterer's business on the corner of Mundesley Road. In his younger days, however, he was a baker's roundsman for Mr. Fayers, an occupation in which, with his horse and cart, he visited a large number of the outlying villages. It was, furthermore, a time when every cottager made his own home-brewed wine from all sorts of natural ingredients which were readily available in the countryside – and it was really strong stuff! Young Jack was very popular with his customers and, if he had a fault, it was that he could never say "No" to the offer of a little drop of refreshment. Thus, there were times when he had a glass of wine at just about every cottage at which he called, with the result that, after making his final call, he would climb into his cart and fall fast asleep. This, however, presented no problem, for the horse immediately knew that it was its job to take him home. It was quite a long way, probably four or five miles, and the horse became a familiar sight as it carried its human cargo through Banningham and Felmingham and into the town, where it would stop outside the house until Jack woke up.

Jack was by no means unique in this habit, for it was repeated in many towns and villages throughout the countryside. There was, indeed, a parallel in East Runton, where a certain gentleman was in the habit of travelling with his pony and trap into Cromer every Saturday to spend the evening in one of the local hostelries. At closing time he would fall asleep and the pony would take him home. He, however, was not as fortunate as Jack in North Walsham for, on one fateful night, a member of the local constabulary happened to be in the vicinity of the Runton Road and he spotted the apparently driverless pony and trap scooting along the coast road at quite a steady pace. He decided that the matter needed investigating and, jumping on his bicycle, he pedalled off in hot pursuit. After quite a chase, he overhauled the vehicle and, bringing the pony to a halt, beheld the vision of our friend sound asleep in the trap. The miscreant received a rude awakening and was duly presented with a summons to appear before the magistrates at Cromer on the following Tuesday. There he was charged with being "in charge of a horse and carriage whilst under the influence of alcohol", for which he was duly fined the sum of half-a-crown. This was by no means the end of the story, however, for the same thing happened the following week and he was again fined half-a-crown. Even then, it seems that he was unable, or perhaps unwilling, to change the habit of a lifetime and the same little drama was played out week after week. Indeed, it became such a saga that a certain wag of the time suggested that it might be worth his while asking the magistrate if he could have a season ticket. The great thing about this story is that, unlike so many of the old tales, every detail has been duly preserved for posterity in the records of the proceedings of Cromer Magistrates' Court.

Reverting to Jack Hall, it must be said that, as a florist, a certain amount of his trade was carried on in public houses, particularly on Sunday mornings. All classes of society were sticklers for convention and, on that day, all men wore their Sunday-best suits with the added adornment of a floral buttonhole. At the back of his shop, Jack had a greenhouse in which he grew such things as carnations and camellias, and he would make these up into buttonholes and sell them to the Sunday morning drinkers for something like four-pence or sixpence. I suppose there was no reason why this aspect of his business should have taken up the entire morning, but Jack tended to linger and, perhaps, was himself "button-holed" into sharing refreshment with his customers.

It was not only flowers that Jack Hall sold, however, for he also provided a wide variety of fruit, as well as cigarettes, sweets and seeds. Then there was his own home-made ice cream, which he usually started making in May or June (we never had ice cream in the winter) and which we collected from his shop in enamel mugs. He was a hard worker and he expected the same quality from others, not least his young daughter Ethel, who helped in all matters connected with the business. It was an age when nothing was ever wasted, and Ethel spent many long hours making cone-shaped sweet bags out of pages from the Parish Magazine or the "Young Soldier". But it was probably when there was a death in the community that they were at their busiest. The loss of one of its members was felt throughout the community and, when the funeral cortege passed through the town on its slow journey to the cemetery, everybody and every vehicle on the streets stood motionless while it went by. Men's caps were doffed and heads were bowed as a mark of respect. Furthermore, there would always be as many as thirty or more wreaths, and it was these which had kept Jack busy for many a long hour.

To begin with, he would carefully remove the wire from empty orange boxes, and it was this that he used to make the framework which would mould the shape of the wreath. This was then packed with moss, and it is here that Ethel's share of the work played its part, for she was periodically despatched out into the countryside to collect it from the hedgebanks. She would take a couple of sacks with her and, when these were full, she would stand them in some pre-arranged spot for later collection by her father with his horse and cart. Then, with all the basic requirements available, Jack would work solidly at his task for many hours and, all the while, a Woodbine hung from his lips. It was said, in fact, that, when he had finished a long session, he appeared to be several inches taller because of the great pile of short ends on which he stood.

On completion of the work, there then came the matter of delivering the wreaths, and once again Ethel was called in to help. If there were not too many they could manage the task on their bicycles, but usually the horse and cart became necessary. It was then that Ethel faced the worst part of the entire business, for there were no chapels of rest and it was the custom for the deceased to be laid out behind closed curtains in the front parlour. Furthermore, convention decreed that all callers at the house should go through to pay their last respects and, in the case of a woman, this involved giving the deceased a final kiss. Poor little Ethel lost count of the number of times she was required to carry out this formality, but it remains vividly etched in her memory.

A recent conversation with Ethel revealed yet another convention of which, previously, I had no knowledge. It concerned the actual colour of wreaths for, whereas today they are to be seen in every imaginable hue, custom in the early part of the century decreed that the accepted colours for a man were white and mauve, whilst for a woman it was white with either pink or lemon. It seems that, even in death, our forefathers were governed by the conventions of the day.

CHAPTER 10
Windmills and Wherries.

It used to be said that if you have never seen a windmill and a wherry, then you have never been to Norfolk. That, however, was a long time ago and it is highly probable that many visitors to this county of ours see nothing of either, unless it be the crumbling remains of the former. Like the horse, windmills have steadily fallen victim to the power of the engine, although a pleasing number are being saved and restored to their earlier majesty by preservation societies and enthusiastic individuals. Thus it is possible for a generation who never knew them in their working days to get some idea of what conditions were like when the sails were turning and the stones grinding. Even these, however, do not tell the full story, for it was not possible for the old-time miller to maintain the degree of light and cleanliness which now greets the visitor.

Clifford Temple, that renowned chronicler of times past, recalls a visit he once paid to an old working mill when conditions inside were far from inviting. The miller followed him as they began their climb past the apple-wood wheel, the wallower and the grinding stones and up into the higher recesses of the mill. It was then that, looking up, he saw what appeared to be hundreds of tiny electric lights glowing in the semi-darkness, and he enquired of the miller as to their purpose. "Lights?" said the miller. "They aren't ruddy lights". Clifford cringed in horror as he suddenly became aware that they were, in fact, the eyes of hundreds of rats reflecting the little light from the top of the mill as they watched his every move.

It was the coming of the railway which signalled the demise of the wherries, though some of them were "a long time a-dying". One of my early boyhood memories is of sitting on the river bank in the gathering dusk of evening and watching three loaded wherries, in line astern, stealthily making their way along the silent waterway. We will never see the like again. Now, the North Walsham to Dilham canal stands still, with its silted waters serving merely as a memorial to a golden age of sail.

Kelling Mill, demolished 1934.

Youngman's Mill, North Walsham, demolished 1902.

It was all so very different when the Canal had opened in 1826, for it brought our part of the River Ant into direct navigable contact with the rest of Norfolk's waterways. For the first time, 14-ton wherries were able to make the journey from Wayford Bridge right through to Antingham Ponds, where Ted Horsfield carried on the calling of Bone Crusher in partnership with my great, great uncle, George Bagshaw. It had taken an Act of Parliament to bring the Canal into being, and five locks were necessary to control the flow of water. Sadly, that flow was never sufficient to allow more than three wherries to sail in either direction each day, so the Canal can hardly be described as a resounding success. Nevertheless, the North Walsham miller, Edward Press, bought it from the Canal Company and went into partnership with Charlie Pallett, thus founding what was to become a long-standing Town business.

I must confess that, in our boyhood days, we gave little thought to the commercial viability of the Canal but regarded it merely as a playground where we could spend Sunday afternoons and Summer evenings. Already, the wherries went no further than Bacton Wood Mill, and that is where my friend Billy and I were often to be found. There, it was possible to hire a boat for sixpence an hour, and it was there, also, that Josh Wells, a Salvation Army Ensign who lived at Swafield, hired out a donkey and cart for the same price. This was of no interest to us, however, for we never had that amount of money to spare. We were content to wander along the banks, finding joy in watching the activities of sticklebacks and swallowtails and the wealth of other wild species which abounded in that idyllic spot. When we grew bigger and owned bicycles, we derived much excitement from pedalling at full speed over the hump-backed bridge for, at the apex, we literally took off and landed with a bump on the other side. We ran the risk of meeting a horse and cart coming up the other side, but we always got away with it, for there was little traffic in those days.

Some of our more adventurous colleagues found their fun by swimming in the Canal, and a few of the more daredevil characters delighted in diving into the waters of the locks. This practice was not without its inherent dangers and most of the participants made sure that their parents were unaware of the manner in which they were spending their leisure time. One of my friends, Harry Hendry, was unable to prevent the secret from reaching the ears of his mother, who was understandably aghast at the very thought of it and tried to dissuade him from engaging in such a dangerous sport. Harry was very stubborn, however, and, despite maternal pleas, insisted that it was not only good fun but also perfectly safe. Mrs. Hendry, having no choice other than to accept defeat, finally yielded.

"All right", she said. "Do you go. But, do you come home drowned, I shan't half give you a thacking!"

It was a wonderful example of the gift which so many Norfolk people possessed of using the wrong words and yet still making their point. I am reminded, in a different context, of the day when the first traffic lights came to North Walsham. One of the town's great characters at that time was old Billy Thirtle, who was always to be seen around the town with his pony and trap. On the day in question, the lights were duly installed and switched on for the first time. Little groups of men stood around and watched as the red, orange and green lights, so brilliant in their pristine freshness, shone forth like beacons. Then, who should be the first person to drive along and be controlled by them but Billy and his pony and trap. As he approached, the vivid red light gave out its message. Billy looked at it, but he paid it no heed and proceeded to drive straight through.

"Hey, Billy", shouted one of the bystanders. "You've just committed an offence".

"That I hin't", replied Billy. "Them lights don't appeal to me. They only appeal to motors".

But we must return to the wherries. I suppose the sight of the beautifully restored *Albion* stealing almost silently around the Norfolk waterways may well conjure up an image of an idyllic existence, with Skipper and Mate sharing the peace and tranquillity of the Broadland scene with only the wildlife which surrounded them. There may well have been times when that was a true picture but, for the most part, the life of a wherryman was by no means an easy one, and it needed a special breed of man to take on the job. Handling those majestic craft was a skilled occupation. Wherrymen knew every inch of the waterways and, even more significantly, they knew the capabilities of their craft. Aided by a fair wind, there were not too many problems but, in foul weather, it was a question of toughness and endurance. Then, in the hard winters of those days, there were times when the waters froze for weeks, or even months, on end. Then all water transport came to a halt, and that meant no pay for the wherryman. Even at such times, however, there were sometimes compensations, and an old wherryman told me of the time when Jack Powley, the early skipper of the *Albion*, skated all the way from Bungay to Beccles on the frozen waters of the Waveney.

Summer brought more diversions, for every centre had its regatta or water frolic, and there were always races for wherries. One site of such revelry was Barton Broad, where the annual August Bank Holiday Regatta has taken place for well over a hundred years. In the early days it was organised by farmers from around the Stalham area, who looked upon it as an excuse for a good day out. Indeed, as the yachting correspondent of the "Eastern Daily Press" said in 1926, "Barton owes much of its popularity to the fact that the racing is a mere incident and that the day has a strongly marked social side. Barton, in fact, is just a picnic and the jolliest one imaginable".

The farmers certainly looked upon it in that light for, on board the wherry which served as a committee boat, they always had "the traditional Stalham salt beef, a barrel of beer and a cheese for lunch". To complete the atmosphere, Stalham Town Band, from a lighter moored among the reeds, played selections from their repertoire. One suspects that the wherrymen looked upon their race as a serious matter, however, for, in the early days, as many as thirteen took part, which must have presented certain

Briggate Lock.

Dilham Lock.

103

A lone wherry steals across Barton Broad.

difficulties on the starting line. One delightful touch which evoked the spirit of the age was that, as the first wherry crossed the finishing line, the band struck up with "See the Conquering Hero Comes".

Gradually the number of wherries declined until, in 1926, there were just four – the *Ella* (our local boat from North Walsham), the *Stalham Trader,* the *Lord Roberts* and, the "conquering hero" on that occasion, the *Hilda.* It is now many years since there was a wherry race at Barton, but there is one representative of the breed who makes her way there on every August Bank Holiday to serve as the committee boat. She is, of course, the grand old *Albion,* who stands serenely surveying the scene where, in successive years in 1891 and 1892, she was sprightly enough to be first across the finishing line.

Over the years the programme of races has altered in line with the changing face of boating. The motor boat race, in which there was one class for under 10 m.p.h. and another for over 10 m.p.h. has now, not surprisingly, gone. Still remaining, however, are two of the traditional old races – one for boats from the River Ant and another which is best described as for all-comers, being open to yachts of any shape, size and rig.

We never knew *Albion* in her old working days, for she was a Bungay-based craft and spent most of her time gliding along the marsh-bordered waters of the Waveney, across the wilderness of Breydon Water and into Yarmouth. We had heard of Breydon, and even of Bungay, but to us they were so far away that they might just as well have been on the other side of the world. We were more familiar with the craft which frequented the waters of "our" river, the Ant. There was the *Lord Roberts* and the *Stalham Trader,* the *Hilda,* and the little fleet which belonged to Barclay and Pallett's, the *Ethne, Elizabeth, Bertha* and *Ella.* The *Ella,* indeed, had the distinction of being the last wherry ever built, coming proudly out of Allen's yard at Coltishall in 1912. Eventually, she was taken over by Nat Bircham of Wroxham, a fine wherryman if ever there was one.

The milling firm of Barclay, Pallett & Co. was a business concern of some size, with their head office in North Walsham and other depots at such places as Wroxham, Cromer, Gunton, Aylsham and Cawston and staithes, of course, at Bacton Wood and Wayford Bridge. Originally known as Press and Pallett, it later became Pallett and Barclay and eventually, when Colonel Barclay of Hanworth Hall came on the scene, he gave his family name prior place in the title. There were several of us, incidentally, who wished we could have gained admittance to the Colonel's estate, for its 200-acre park was crammed with vast numbers of forest trees, including a Spanish Oak which was said to be 300 years old and measured forty feet around the trunk. We would dearly have loved to inspect this magnificent specimen but, unfortunately, we didn't really move in such elevated circles.

One man who vividly remembers life on the old working wherries is Ben Scott who, when not delivering coal for Barclay and Pallett's, was mate on the *Bertha* with Skipper Bates of Coltishall. Ben and his skipper built up a detailed knowledge of the waterways of that part of Norfolk, for their cargoes were varied in the extreme and could frequently require them to venture along dykes leading simply to an individual farm, house or mill. Coal was a frequent cargo in the days before the coming of the railway; corn was taken to the various mills and the resultant flour later brought back; timber and hay, sugar beet and marsh litter – the list was almost endless. Reeds were carried to Wayford Bridge, from where, in later times, the journey was completed on lorries to Mr. Farman, the thatcher. Pig iron was transported to Swafield Wharf on its way

Reed Gathering at Fleet Dyke, South Walsham.

to Randell's foundry in Bacton Road. There was, incidentally, one Norwich wherry called the *Adam and Eve* and owned by Mrs. Howes, who kept the hostelry of the same name, which was employed solely in carrying sand for the floors of Norwich public houses.

Much of the work of the wherry was carried out in shallow waters, for which its design was admirably suited. In deeper water, however, her sailing qualities could be improved by the use of a unique feature known as a "slipping keel". This was a false wooden keel which could be fitted below the normal keel, and Ben described it to me in great detail. When this keel was fitted, it had to be precisely manoeuvred under the wherry and then three plugs were removed from the original keel. The false one was brought quickly into place and then secured by bolts through the three plug holes. This called for a high degree of precision from the two crew members for, as soon as the plugs were removed, water started entering the boat. It used to be said, however, that it was a poor wherryman who allowed more than a couple of bucketfuls of water to find its way aboard during the operation.

The broadland waters were havens of peace in those days, and there were people ashore who were beginning to express an interest in using them for holiday purposes. Thus it was that the *Bertha* was called upon to carry a human cargo, and Ben Scott and Skipper Bates set to work with a will to make their vessel suitable for carrying guests. A good scrub was the first requirement, followed by an improvement in facilities for the benefit of those who were willing to pay for the privilege of sailing in her. The tiny cabin provided only rudimentary accommodation for the crew, for wherries were never used by families as floating homes in the manner of the canal narrowboats. Thus the remainder of the boat had to be transformed, beginning with bunks and (something the crew never enjoyed) a portable toilet. Ben completed the picture for me by describing how they would then take on board one of those old gramophones with the familiar large horn and, finally, a piano. It was, of course, an age when music was a vital constituent of life, and the coming guests did not wish to be deprived of the traditional songs round the piano which were such a feature of life in the average home.

The increasing interest in the Broads for holiday purposes led to the development of the wherry yacht, built purely for pleasure purposes. A recently-discovered advertisement of 1907 informs us that, at that time, a party of eight could have hired a wherry for a week for the sum of £14. The cost of provisions ("best hamper, including fresh-cooked meat") would have set the party back another £10, with what were described as "incidental expenses on shore" adding a further £4. Thus the total cost for eight people would have been £28, representing no more than £3.10.0d for each person. In contrast, one of those old wherries, having recently been saved from a watery grave and lovingly restored, is currently on offer at £1,000 per week. In fairness, however, it should be added that this grand old lady now offers rather more in the way of facilities than the holidaymaker of 1907 could have expected, including galley, engine room and the added luxury of two showers.

But, to return to the banks of the Canal, where Bacton Wood Mill stood sentinel over the scene, just as a mill is reputed to have done on that very spot since the time of the Domesday Book. We were not aware, at that time, that we were witnessing the end of an era, but so it was to be. By 1935 the last trading wherries were only reaching as far as Ebridge Mill, and the approaching war was to see the end of a Victorian enterprise which foundered on the rock of progress. It is rumoured, indeed, that it was the local Home Guard who unwittingly drove the last nail into the coffin of that little stretch of canal.

When the Canal had been built, gulleys had been laid along the sides to prevent flooding and, at one point, the gulley had been driven underneath the bottom of the waterway. At some time or other, as the Canal gradually silted up and became overgrown, a metal oil drum had become wedged in this subterranean passage, and the Home Guard decided to remove it. It is possible that it could have been dealt with by normal physical means, but they, being a military organisation, decided to bring their specialised skills into play by using an explosive charge. The operation was highly successful, for the oil drum was never seen again. It was merely unfortunate that, when the charge exploded, it also blew a hole in the bottom of the Canal! Anyway, that is the story I was told, although I have not yet discovered anybody willing to admit to having been a witness to the operation.

Perhaps the time may come when that little waterway is again opened up as a living reminder of the stately old craft which plied the Broadland waters and made their way up to Antingham Bone Mill. Nostalgia, they say, doesn't pay the rent. But, then, if the Norfolk Wherry Trust had viewed it that way, the world would not now be treated to the sight of the *Albion* making her way around the rivers where she first earned a living before the turn of the century.

CHAPTER 11

"Merely Players".

All the world, we are told, is a stage, and each of us, as we make our brief passage across its boards, plays a part in the steady succession of dramas and comedies which unfold around us. The cast list is a big one, however, and it falls to very few of us to achieve stardom and the fame which goes with it. Most of us are destined to be merely small fishes in a big pond, quickly forgotten when we make our final exit into the wings, except, perhaps, by those who loved us while we were here. We are the "bit" players in the Theatre of Life.

Similarly, not many of us enjoy the privilege of associating with the personalities whose names head the list of characters. We read about them but, even in the case of those we admire, they never become real people. Sometimes this is just as well for, all too often, they are revealed as little more than paper gods. The only people we really know are those with whom we spend our daily lives and, over the years, their numbers become legion. Looking back over a lifetime spent in the countryside of Norfolk, one recalls a multitude of ordinary people leading ordinary lives, and among them there are many who made life the richer simply by being there. To chronicle them all would be impossible and I must satisfy myself by remembering just three widely-differing men who were "merely players".

The first of my trio, it must be admitted, did have an unwelcome fame thrust upon him in his later years but, in spite of that, he always remained true to his humble beginnings. It was George Edwards, whom I met just once and, if it had been anybody but my father who had told me that he was a Member of Parliament, I would have found it difficult to believe. Admittedly I was only nine years old and the round-shouldered little man was around 80, not many years away from the end of his life. Then there was the fact that I had only ever met one other M.P., and that was Tom Cook from Sennowe Park, a very different figure. But George Edwards just didn't look the way I thought an M.P. was supposed to look. In my own defence I can only say that I was too young to have

109

known what had brought about that hunched back, that sallow complexion and that shuffling walk.

It was only later, by talking to people who had known him and, even more, by reading his autobiography, that I became aware of the way in which he had overcome misfortune to become a man of true greatness. After all, had he not, when only five years old, seen his father sent to prison for stealing five turnips because there was no bread in the house? Had he not then spent the winter of 1855 in the workhouse with his mother and his six brothers and sisters? And had he not then gone scaring crows from sunrise to sunset for a shilling a week, only to receive a thrashing and a deduction of twopence when the farmer found him asleep in the hedgerow?

Born in 1850, George Edwards faced a life of hardship and deprivation such as can hardly be imagined in today's society. Indeed, many politicians who talk glibly about present-day poverty might benefit from a study of what the word meant to agricultural workers and others at the turn of the century. Working on the land almost as soon as he could walk, the young George had received no education worth talking about and, even when he got married at the age of 22, he could neither read nor write. It was then that his new wife came to the rescue, however, for she had acquired both skills and proceeded to pass them on to him with the aid of the Bible and a Methodist hymn book. From then on, there was no stopping him as he sought to improve his knowledge and to emulate the achievements of such figures as Keir Hardie and Joseph Arch.

It was at a meeting at the Angel Hotel in North Walsham on July 6th 1906 that he brought into being the Eastern Counties Agricultural Labourers' and Smallholders' Union, later to be known as the National Union of Agricultural Workers. He was, above all, a man of great courage and he feared nobody, irrespective of their position in society. When he won a seat on Norfolk County Council, he stood up to both Liberals and Tories and won not only their respect but also their friendship.

Then, in 1922, when he was 72 years old, he achieved the greatest success of his life. Standing for the Labour Party, he won the election for the South Norfolk constituency, thereby becoming the first farm labourer to occupy a seat in the House of Commons. He had come a long way since that early winter in the workhouse, but life was still not without its problems, the most urgent being that of how to dress when he took his seat. It was well remembered

MR. G. EDWARDS M.P. WITH HIS AGENT.
AFTER THE COUNTING 2118 MAJORITY.

THRKES
9 CHESTER ST
NORWICH

111

that Keir Hardie had earlier flouted convention by arriving in a cloth cap and tweed suit, but the House still clung to the tradition of top hats and frock coats. George Edwards respected that tradition, but he still felt that a top hat for a farm labourer would be too much of a sham. He settled for the tall, flat-topped bowler which had been so popular. Even then, the hardest part still lay ahead of him. I feel that I can do no better than quote his own words as they appear in "From Crow-Scaring to Westminster", thus:

"From the Monday to the Wednesday morning I had not fully realised that I was actually a Member of Parliament. It was brought home to me, however, when I had to get ready to proceed to London, and then, strange as it may seem, instead of being full of joy, I actually broke down with the deepest emotion. I cannot account for it, but it was so, and the first words that I could utter were a desire that my poor dear wife could know. I also offered a fervent prayer that God would keep me humble, and that I might always remain the same George Edwards, the agricultural labourer. This might appear to be approaching very near to cant, but it was sincere, and I have tried to live it out".

George Edwards continued to "live it out", in spite of the award of a knighthood and an O.B.E., until that day in 1933 when he made his last journey from the Methodist Chapel to the Cemetery in Fakenham.

The second character from my past is Gilbert Hewitt, with whom I first became acquainted when we both began our education at North Walsham Council School. Our association was somewhat spasmodic and, even in our schooldays, I cannot claim to have known Gilly Hewitt really well, for he was rather senior to me and, at that stage of one's development, even three years can form an almost unbridgeable barrier to close friendship. Then, as we advanced towards adulthood, our paths took us in different directions and our relationship was intermittent. This is a matter of some regret to me, for Gilly was the sort of person who could make life seem brighter by his mere presence.

He became a hairdresser by profession but, throughout his life, his every waking moment was filled with thoughts of angling. He lived and breathed fishing and, as his wife put it, "Westwick Lake was his second home". Rarely did the conversation in his salon range over any other topic, and there were countless youngsters who benefitted from the help and advice which he so readily dispensed. Furthermore, it was not only the fishing which he loved, but also the surroundings in his favourite waterside haunts. There were the trees coming down to the water's edge, the ripple of the wind in the leaves and, of course, the song of the birds. He was a true nature lover; indeed, it could be said that he was a conservationist almost before the word was invented. Wednesday was always early closing day in North Walsham, but Gilly went one better by closing all day. By that means he was able to get to one of his favourite haunts and spend the night fishing.

A friend of mine who frequently accompanied him on those nocturnal trips, and who told me much about the real Gilly Hewitt, was Peter Hooker. I know little about the finer points of angling and I asked Peter how on earth they managed to see their floats in the darkness. Peter replied that it was no real problem, for they used a special night float which had in the top a small phial of a gas called tritium which was visible in the darkness. At one stage, however, Peter found difficulty in seeing his float, and it was then that Gilly produced a more efficient version. He devised what became known as the "Norfolk Gilly Hewitt Float", which had two light sources on the top and which made the float visible for as far as anybody could cast his line. Peter proudly showed me a couple of these floats, which I believe have now become somewhat rare.

Peter also told me the story of one disastrous night in the middle of Heigham Sound when the pair of them teamed up with Peter's nephew, Ray Cutting, to form a threesome. It looked like being a successful expedition, for the bream were running well and they were soon landing them almost as quickly as they could cast. They were using a 12-foot keepnet, held in place by a stick wedged under one of the seats of the boat, and into that net went a steady succession of nice fat bream. Before long, they reached the point where, in Peter's estimation, there must have been somewhere between 200 and 250 pounds of fish in the net. It was then, however, that disaster struck as one of the party (I believe it was Peter) added yet another fish to the collection. It proved to be the proverbial straw that broke the camel's back, for it was sufficient to cause the stick to become dislodged from under the seat and the keepnet to disappear below the surface of the water. Drastic action was then called for and Peter, grabbing the gaff, made frantic efforts to hook the net and bring it back. Eventually, with great relief, he succeeded and hauled it up from the depths. Sadly, however, he had hooked the bottom end of the net, with the result that the greater part of their massive catch had an early escape back into the waters of Heigham Sound. Peter looked quite sad as he related this story to me but, as I suggested to him, at least it gave the three of them a true story to tell of the ones that got away.

It was Peter Hooker who also introduced me to another face of Gilbert Hewitt – that of the Poet. I had known that Gilly had jotted down lines of verse at odd times, but I had never realised the quality of his work until Peter produced a few sheets of paper which he kept as a little memento of his old friend. The poem which I have chosen to reproduce here is not only touching in its almost childlike simplicity but will also, I believe, paint a far better picture of the man than could ever come from my pen. He calls it "An Old Man's Prayer".

Lord, you know there's times I've not been good,
But I've always tried hard to be.
I'd try even harder if you could prepare
A spot in your Heaven for me.
Just supposing, then – could you not plan
That my life in your Heaven might be
Like this life down here, so that I can go
A-fishing when it pleases me.
And could I choose the setting and scene
Which would give me much peace and great joy,
Then I would choose the lake of my dreams,
The place where I fished, man and boy.
The trees sweep down to shelter the shore,
Where there's good swims, some shallow, some deep,
And the tench run eight or nine pounds and more
And monster carp roll, slap and leap.
Where my float will lift and glide away,
And my old rod strike quickly to bend
Into fish that lunge and fight all day,
Yet will come to the net in the end.

But, Lord, if behind your Heaven's door
There aren't any lakes, fish or trees,
I won't like it, Lord. No. And, what's more,
I would rather stay here if you please.

Sorry, Lord, it's not just the fishing,
It's the sun and the moon and the rain,
The wind in the trees and the song of the birds,
And the magic when Spring comes again.
And I've a million more reasons, dear Lord,
For wishing my three score and ten
Were the number of seasons that I could fish through
All over again, Lord. Amen.

Sadly, Gilbert Hewitt died much too soon but, in accordance with his wish, his ashes were scattered on the waters of one of his favourite haunts. Whenever I pass near that spot I rejoice in the thought that he now rests where, in life, he found peace and contentment.

Records indicate that, over the years, North Walsham has been served by something like thirty inns, taverns and other hostelries, of which only a handful now remain. Some of the older ones, such as the White Lion and the Maid's Head, which stood around the Market Place, and the Boar where, every Thursday, the Petty Sessions were held, have been long forgotten. Others, like the Dog, the Red Lion and the Mitre Tavern, exist only in the memory, the last-named only because of the activities which went on in the yard which surrounded it.

In my boyhood there remained perhaps fourteen such hostelries and of those, because of my tender years, I had little direct knowledge. I knew the Angel and the Orchard Gardens as places where my father played bowls. Then there was the Blue Bell, where such men as Bob Scott and George Wright supplemented their income by curing herrings, and near which, one dark and tragic night, old Billy Goose came to an untimely end in the tadpole pond. The two which most sparked my imagination, however, were the Black Swan and the King's Arms, for it was still the age of the horse, and both had close associations in that respect. Both had been posting houses and each had been successively under the proprietorship of the Palmer family.

Robert Walpole Palmer was a man who lived and breathed horses, and he was supported in this by his wife, formerly Alice Bacon, whose family had kept livery stables in Norwich since 1822. It was a time when the horse was still king on the roads of Norfolk, just as it was on the farms, and the Palmers hired out horses and

An early coach party leaving the Angel Hotel, North Walsham.

A more modern coach party leaving the White Swan.

carriages of all sorts, as well as acting as carting agents to the Great Eastern Railway Company. They also employed Billy Sole to "drive the flies away from the railway station", an occupation which struck me as being somewhat odd until I realised that the flies in question were the old horse cabs in which prospective patrons were transported to the King's Arms. It was also the time when the coastal resorts of Cromer and Sheringham, Mundesley and Overstrand were becoming fashionable and to these the Palmers ran a fleet of horse buses, rather like stage coaches. At that time the number of horses in their stables and paddocks totalled two hundred, and it was into this world that, in 1893, their son Frank had been born.

It was, I think, inevitable that young Frank should ride almost as soon as he could walk and, as he got older, he went everywhere on horseback. Before long, he was riding as a trumpeter for the Norfolk Imperial Yeomanry, which had been formed by Major Barclay of Hanworth Hall. Then came the Great War and one would have expected him to join the cavalry. It was not so, however, for he immediately began service in the Royal Flying Corps, the reason being that those early flying machines needed a horseman's hands to control them. They were not flown by means of buttons and switches and it needed all the sensitivity of a horseman to master their unpredictable habits. It was towards the end of the War that Frank Palmer, together with two of his fellow officers, attended the funeral of Baron Richtofen, the German air ace, after he had been shot down in 1918. One suspects that, even in war, he most probably derived a certain pleasure from showing that little touch of chivalry to his old adversary.

After the war, he did not return to North Walsham but, instead, took over the livery stables of his uncle, Robert Bacon, at the Barn Tavern in Norwich. One of his first actions was to pay off all the outstanding accounts so that he could, in his own words, "start off with a clean slate". To this end, he went across the road to the wheelwright who regularly carried out work for his uncle, and explained the purpose of his visit. The wheelwright took him to a corner of the workshop where there lay a pile of planks of wood and, selecting one of the planks, held it up. There on the face of the wood, written in pencil, was the name BACON and, underneath, a list of jobs which had been done, together with the respective charges. Frank settled up the account and then tentatively suggested that he might have a receipt.

"Receipt?" said the wheelwright. "You don't need no receipt", and, with that, he picked up a plane and planed the wood clean. Then, taking a pencil from behind his ear, he wrote across the top the name PALMER ."There you are", he said. "Now we can make a fresh start".

So, Captain Frank Bacon Palmer, to give him his full title, went about his business of hiring out horses for riding and carriages for such things as weddings and funerals. He even had a small cart in which he took some of his younger clients to and from school, frequently with some of the local urchins jumping on the back for a free ride. Then, as horses went into decline as working animals, he concentrated on teaching riding at his stables at Harford Bridges, together with organising frequent gymkhanas in aid of the Animal Health Trust. It was, in fact, at one of these events that I met him for the first time for, although we had both attended the same school, he was nearly thirty years my senior. I soon found that he exactly fitted the description given to me by my father, who knew him well – the sly sense of humour and the obvious love of both horses and children. He had no time for doting parents who encouraged their offspring to learn to ride simply for the purpose of collecting rosettes and, above all, he could not tolerate cruelty to animals. He proceeded to give me a lengthy description of his methods of training horses, but I have to admit that there is now only one sentence of that long discourse which I can recall.

"You'll never train a horse by hitting it", he said, "but it's surprising what you can do with a lump of sugar".

That was horse lore in the Palmer tradition and, as a kind of post-script, I conclude with one last story concerning his father. It was when the old man was confined to his bed with what was to prove to be his last illness, and he was becoming steadily weaker as he declined all offers of food. His nurse, in desperation, tried her hardest to tempt him into taking some nourishment.

"Now, come along", she said. "I want you to take some of my calves' foot jelly. I've kept patients going for weeks on calves' foot jelly".

"That's nothing", replied the old man. "Do you go down to the stables and take a look at my horse 'Sugar'. I've kept him going for twenty years on mild beer and Woodbines".

CHAPTER 12

Maritime Yarmouth.

It was on an October day in the very early thirties that Great Yarmouth and I first became acquainted. I have always thought it to be fortunate that I should have had my first contact with the town at that time of the year, for only then does one become aware of the true heartbeat of the place rather than the somewhat artificial image which it adopts in order to please the annual influx of summer visitors. On that autumn day when I paid my first call, the holidaymakers, having packed away their "kiss-me-quick" hats and assorted specimens of Mr. Docwra's Yarmouth Rock, had taken their leave and returned to their real world in London and the Midlands. In their place had come other visitors, men and women who were not attracted there by candy floss and amusement arcades, but by one simple thing – the herring.

It was the heyday of the herring industry and every year the ritual was repeated. In May, the drifters would congregate off the Shetland Islands ready for the first appearance of the fish, and then there would be the steady progress down the east coast of Scotland and northern England, until the shoals arrived off the East Anglian coast in the autumn. Yarmouth was the greatest herring port in Britain and as many as a thousand drifters, local and Scottish, took part in the autumn run. News of their approach would spread through the town, and crowds of people would throng the piers to watch the skippers ease their vessels into the harbour mouth and tie up at the quayside. Before long, the river was a solid mass of boats and it was possible to walk on their decks from one bank to the other. This was particularly so on Sundays for, although the local men had no qualms about fishing on the Sabbath, nothing would induce the Scots to forego their religious beliefs on that day.

While the Scottish fishermen were bringing their drifters into harbour, another influx of visitors was taking place at the railway station in the form of their womenfolk, whose job it was to gut and pack the herring. The Scots Fisher Girls (or "lassies") were a brawny bunch of Amazons who came in their hundreds from such places as Banff, Buckie, Fraserburgh and Stornaway and transformed the

The fishing fleet arrives at Yarmouth for the start of the herring season.

Fishing boats leaving Gorleston harbour.

atmosphere of the town in more ways than one. My own first sight of them created a strong feeling of surprise for, though they were always referred to as girls, it was immediately apparent that many of them were old enough to be my mother and, in many cases, even my grandmother. Their clothing was mainly dark in colour, with thick skirts and seamen's jerseys, scarves round their heads and, in the cold weather, shawls over their shoulders to complete the ensemble. Then, with long knitting needles tucked under their arms and balls of wool in their apron pockets, they knitted with incredible speed as they walked around the town. One could hear their approach from a distance, partly by the sound of their heavy boots but mainly because of their seemingly never-ending chatter. Their unusual Gaelic speech fell strangely upon our ears and, when they sporadically burst into song, the sound had a somewhat primitive quality about it. Above all, however, they carried the aroma of their calling wherever they went, and it was not every landlady who was willing to offer them accommodation.

My first visit to the Court of King Herring had been arranged by my parents as part of a scheme to widen my knowledge in preparation for my forthcoming scholarship exam. Far from being a mere educational chore, however, it proved such a fascination that I returned on every possible occasion. Now, looking back on those halcyon days, it is difficult to recall which aspect of the industry made the greatest impact on my young mind. I had, of course, seen a lot of the fishermen of Cromer and Sheringham, but the hurly-burly of the Yarmouth quayside was like a different world.

Few who have ever seen the steady line of drifters putting to sea will readily forget the way in which each in succession would rise to meet the swell at the harbour bar. Then, after a hard night seeking out the Silver Darlings, they would return, heavily laden, in a mad dash to unload as quickly as possible in the hope of gaining the highest prices. It was what followed next, however, which aroused in me the greatest feeling of excitement. Cran after cran was lifted from the hold and dropped on the quay, the auctioneer's bell would ring, and both fish and men seemed to be everywhere whilst, up above, seagulls wheeled and screeched in the hope of a succulent meal. It was all conducted in accordance with a long-established routine but, to the uninitiated, it seemed sheer bedlam.

A short distance away, standing at a row of huge shallow troughs, the Fisher Girls went to work on that part of the catch which was destined for export. With their fingers separately

The Scots Fisher Girls.

bandaged for protection and wearing large black oilskin aprons, they split and gutted the herring and then, without even looking round, flung each one backwards with unerring aim into the waiting barrels behind them. They worked at a tremendous pace, each woman being capable of gutting at least a thousand fish in an hour. One could only stand and marvel at the speed and skill of the operation and, as the troughs emptied, so the men poured in more basketsful in a seemingly never-ending supply.

One man with vivid memories of the scene is Trevor Westgate who, having spent his boyhood in the town, thankfully took his sea-faring grandfather's advice ("Don't ever go to sea for a living, boy") and proceeded to grace the world of journalism in the area around the ports of Yarmouth and Lowestóft. I recalled how I had often succeeded in getting as many as twenty herring for a shilling at the quayside, but he did even better – he got them free.

"Urchins of my generation", he said, "needed only a length of stout cord to bring home enough herring to feed the whole family – and the people next door. One end of the cord was passed through the mouth and out through the gills of the first fish picked up, and a simple knot served to hold a dozen or more fish in place as they were slid in like manner down the line. The custom had been going on for more years than anyone could remember, and though we sometimes had to dodge an impatient kick if we got too close to the man tipping the herring being winched ashore into cran baskets, our right to pick up any fish which fell to the quayside was never questioned.

"And what wonderful sights and sounds and smells there were to absorb as part of the process of growing up in such exciting surroundings!"

Neither he nor I realised all those years ago that we were witnessing the beginning of the end of the herring fishing industry. 1913 had been the peak year, with a total of one and a half million crans being landed at the two East Coast ports. When one bears in mind the fact that a cran can contain anything from a thousand to fifteen hundred fish one begins to marvel at the fact that there could have been so many there in the first place. Now, in the town which introduced the world to the Yarmouth bloater and where the herring could be picked up from the quayside by anybody so inclined, the drifter fleets sail no more.

The gradual demise of the fishing industry was undoubtedly a bitter blow to Great Yarmouth, for the town's prosperity has always depended on the success of the port. It was only part of a continuing story, however, for, in the same way that it had been over the centuries, it was merely a question of adapting to changing circumstances. Now, in those same waters where drifters queued to cross the bar, impersonal container ships bring in their metal-bound loads and service vessels ply back and forth to the offshore gas and oil rigs. The demands of industry have taken over in the heartland of Great Yarmouth where, in the days of my boyhood, going to sea was not just a job but, rather, a way of life. But the little port is no stranger to change – it has seen it all before.

There had been the old luggers which, with the wind in their four-cornered sails, had done the fishing before the advent of the steam drifters; then they, in their turn, had succumbed to the superior power of oil and diesel fuel. There had been the elegant old windjammers, coming from all parts of the world and filling the river with a forest of masts as they tied up at the quayside. There were brigs from the coal-producing countries and barques and barquentines bringing timber from Russia and Scandinavia, each one proudly flying its own national flag. A walk along the quayside on a summer evening to view all those stately craft and to hear the strange-sounding chatter of their crews is a memory which is not readily forgotten, but once again it seems that my boyhood was destined to coincide with the end of an era. The East Coast was the last haven of the sailing ship in Britain and it was the period between the two World Wars which, apart from occasional courtesy visits, saw the last appearance of a windjammer at Yarmouth.

One boat which had already disappeared from Yarmouth before I paid my first visit was the lifeboat. There had been three of them in earlier times: the *John Burch*, the surf boat *Duff* (later renamed *Abraham Thomas*) and finally the *Hugh Taylor*. It was in 1919 that the station was closed after almost seventy years of service, but the local influence was by no means lost, for the responsibility for saving life in that area was taken over by the Gorleston station. There followed a long history of dedication and courage which, unbeaten by any other station around our coast, continues to the present day. For fifty years the Gorleston Volunteer Lifeboat *Elizabeth Simpson* was kept busy, for it was said that four out of every five shipwrecks off the British Isles occurred off the coasts of Norfolk and Suffolk. It was during that period that the name of Gorleston's coxswain, William Fleming, became known far and

This Norwegian brig was typical of the old windjammers which once thronged Yarmouth harbour.

William Fleming, Gorleston's lifeboat hero.

Yarmouth's first lifeboat, the *John Burch*.

And the last, the *Hugh Taylor*.

wide. The mere quoting of statistics can never do justice to the courage of the men of the lifeboats. Perhaps it will suffice to say that William Fleming was Gorleston's Henry Blogg.

During the many boyhood hours I spent around the quayside at Yarmouth I became aware of a vast array of shipping, the likes of which I would never have encountered back at Cromer. Both towns had a great dependence on the sea but, because of their differing situations, the contrast could not have been more marked. At Cromer it was the little longshore boats and crabbers, which had to be physically manhandled into the sea. At Yarmouth, however, they came in all shapes and sizes, many of them being, at that time, the biggest ships I had ever seen. There were colliers and heavily-laden timber ships, some with vast areas of sail and others belching steam and smoke. Many came from strange-sounding places in the Baltic and carried romantic names such as *Helga, Gullkroner* and *Svenborg,* though I still recall a Finnish barque with the unlikely name of *Fred.*

Amidst all that cosmopolitan hustle and bustle, however, there was one boat which has lived longest in my memory. I suppose I should admit to a certain streak in my philosophy which tells me that small is beautiful for, in my eyes, the star of the show was always the fussy little wooden paddle tug *United Service.* Indeed, when, one December day in 1939, she made her way down the River Yare to the breaker's yard, it signalled for me the end of yet another era. She was the last of her line and, for nearly seventy years since her birth at North Shields in 1872, she had been one of the maids of all work on which the life of the port had so much depended.

Her principal task had involved towing ships in and out of the crowded port, particularly the large fleet of sailing smacks and luggers which depended upon the tugs at the beginning and end of every trip. Then there were the lifeboats for, prior to the introduction of motors, the old pull-and-sail boats of both Yarmouth and Gorleston relied on the *United Service* to get them into open water. In addition, at a time when wrecks were all too common along the East Coast, there was the occasional call to assist in the salvage of a vessel stranded out on the sandbanks. Nevertheless, her work was not all of a serious nature for in summer, freshly painted and looking her best, she took holidaymakers on sea trips to Scroby Sands or the Lightship. With her dove-grey hull, white paddle boxes and distinctive black and red funnel, she became widely

The *United Service* towing a windjammer into open water . . .

. . . . and taking holidaymakers on a trip to Scroby Sands.

known to the crowds of pleasure-seekers who boarded her at her moorings at the Town Hall Quay.

When the *United Service* started her work at Yarmouth she joined a fleet of six similar vessels, but she was destined to outshine them all. To begin with, the *Star* went to King's Lynn and the *Sailor* went to North Shields. The *Express* and the *Tyne* battled on against the elements for thirty or forty years before each was successively despatched to the breaker's yard. This left just the *Yare* and the *Victoria*, both of which were destined for a watery grave. The *Yare* went down with honour when, in 1927, she was engaged in salvage work on Scroby Sands. She sank after hitting one of the many wrecks which littered the area, but fortunately her crew were rescued by the *Elizabeth Simpson*.

The *Victoria*, however, came to an ignominious end which is also well recorded in the annals of Cromer history. At the time, she was the pride of the fleet and she was regularly engaged in taking holidaymakers on day trips between the two resorts. Off Cromer, she would drop anchor and her passengers would be taken off to spend a few hours in the town. Then, when they had returned aboard, she would turn about and make the return trip to Yarmouth. It was on the 9th August 1888 that, as the captain began manoeuvring his vessel around, she became stuck fast on an underwater obstruction. No amount of effort on his part would free the *Victoria*, nor even an attempt to drag her clear with a traction engine on the shore. The hazard which held the tug in its grasp was, in fact, the Church Rock, claimed by many to be the remains of the old church of Shipden, which the sea had taken into its keeping back in the fourteenth century. The passengers were disembarked and returned to Yarmouth by train and, having been declared a hazard to shipping, the poor old *Victoria* was blown up by officers of Trinity House.

It then fell to the *United Service* to step into the breach and carry passengers on this popular coastal trip until it was discontinued in 1894. Even then, it was to be many years before the proud old paddler was to make her final trip down the River Yare. She well deserves the affectionate place she now holds in the history of the Port of Great Yarmouth.

CHAPTER 13

Men of the Rows.

One feature of Great Yarmouth which held a fascination for me was that amazing conglomeration of alleyways, the Rows, which must surely have been as quaint as anything in England. The town had earlier been surrounded by a huge fortified wall, outside which nobody was allowed to build, and thus the increasing population had to be packed into the limited area within. It was in order to make the best use of the available land that the 145 Rows, running from east to west and densely packed with habitations, were laid out in a pattern which Charles Dickens likened to the bars of a gridiron. In the buildings which lined the rows lived all sections of the community, from bankers and merchants to tradesmen and the more unsavoury characters who abounded at that time.

A few of the rows were laid out on a grander scale than the others and, indeed, Broad Row and Market Row still survive as major shopping thoroughfares. For the most part, however, the system was made up of a maze of passages giving access to the most basic form of living accommodation imaginable. Local inhabitants could find their way around with ease, but strangers to the area soon became hopelessly lost. Indeed, the Press Gangs who scoured the town in earlier years in search of crews for the Navy's ships suffered much frustration as their intended victims escaped into the gloomy maze of alleyways.

For the pedestrian, the surface of many of the rows was hardly ideal, for some were paved with beach pebbles and had open gutters into which every kind of rubbish was thrown. For vehicles there was the added problem of narrowness which made the rows inaccessible to normal forms of wheeled transport, and this led to the development of the unique "troll cart" in which the shafts were set outside the wheels. By this means the driver knew that, if the shafts could get through, the rest of the cart would automatically follow.

It was not until 1804 that the rows were numbered, thus making it possible for visitors to find their way around. Prior to that, they had acquired names derived either from some feature of the row or, perhaps, from one of the more important personages who lived there. Thus there were such as Gurney's Bank Row, Fighting Cock Row and, down by the river, Ferry Boat Row. There was Sarah Martin's Row, bearing the name of the prison worker who devoted her life to helping the inmates of the town gaol. At the other end of the spectrum there was Old Hannah's Row, home of John Hannah who, having murdered his wife in 1813, paid the penalty in the last public hanging in the borough.

But it was Kittywitches Row which probably held most fascination for the youngsters of my time, for it was the narrowest of them all, measuring as little as 27 inches at one point. My cousin, Roy Worton, was one of the lads who derived great pleasure from trying to ride their bicycles through the row without touching the sides. Even today he recalls with satisfaction the occasions when, with a mere fraction of an inch to spare on either side of his handlebars, he accomplished the feat.

It was the very name of Kittywitches Row which intrigued me as much as anything, for it shared that title with the miniature crabs for which, years earlier, I had sought in the stony pools on Cromer beach. I have never succeeded in tracing the origin of the word kitty-witch in either context, but it seems that Row 95 was not without its traditions of witchcraft. It was there, in fact, that Matthew Hopkins, the 17th-century "Witch-finder", sought out some of the sixteen Yarmouth women whom he sent for execution for being "in league with the devil". Nevertheless, whilst relishing the air of mystery conjured up by this story of the row's chequered past, it must be admitted that there is probably more truth in the suggestion that the name is derived from that of a former resident, one Christopher Wyche.

Even after the numbering of the rows there were some which, because of their proud history, still remained better known by the names they formerly bore. Furthermore, there were at least two others which continued to be well remembered, though certainly with no feeling of pride. One of these, which became Row 6, was the former Body Snatchers' Row. It had received its name from the activities of the men who, in the early nineteenth century, raided cemeteries in search of newly-buried bodies, which they would then sell to hospitals in London for teaching and research. A group of these so-called "Resurrection Men" operated from one of the cottages in Row 6 until their activities were discovered and their leader, a man named Vaughan, was imprisoned in the Tolhouse and then sentenced to transportation.

Kittywitches Row.

The other row bearing a name which many would have preferred to forget was Number 2, formerly Black Horse Row. It took its name from a rather unsavoury hostelry which stood at its eastern end, and the only other building of any note was the common lodging house presided over by Jake Holl. The remainder of the row had nothing better to offer and it was those two buildings, indeed, which caused it to find a place in the annals of Yarmouth folklore. Furthermore, there were also just two characters in the strange story of Black Horse Row – a story which unfailingly struck fear into the hearts of listeners when they heard of the events of that fateful Christmas Eve of 1853.

Jake Holl was one of the dregs of society. A great drunken hulk of a man, he paid little heed to the occupants of his lodging house. As long as they could pay the few pence which he demanded for the use of his accommodation, he was content to ignore them. Most of the time he was to be found in the Black Horse, exchanging his takings for the cheap ale which that hostelry provided. It was there, indeed, that he had been for most of that murky, wet Christmas Eve, and the fact that he returned home somewhat earlier than usual was due simply to the fact that he had been thrown out for failing to pay for the ale he had already consumed.

One of his regular lodgers was a feeble little old man, round-shouldered and sallow of complexion, who made a meagre living playing his fiddle and begging in the streets of the town. He was known to all simply as Old Tom, and his apparent lack of skill as a musician was reflected in the mere pittance which he managed to collect each day, usually just sufficient to pay for his bed. Rumour had it, however, that he had at one time been a highly talented musician and had, indeed, moved in the highest circles. In the way that rumours do, this had led to speculation that he had amassed a large sum of money over the years and that he had his hoard hidden away somewhere. Indeed, it was not unknown for local urchins to follow him along the streets of the town and to taunt him with cries of "Miser, miser"!

He looked anything but a wealthy man, however, as he made his weary way back to the lodging house in Black Horse Row on that fateful Christmas Eve. It had been a tiring day, but much worse was to follow as he opened the door and stumbled inside, for there, waiting for him, was Jake Holl. Still in a drunken fury, Jake had decided that Old Tom would be the source of the money he needed to clear his debts at the Black Horse. Immediately, he seized

133

the little man and demanded gold from his hidden hoard. In vain, Old Tom denied having such a hoard and even offered the lodging house keeper the pittance which he had managed to collect that day. This merely brought forth such sinister threats from his drunken attacker that the little fiddler began to fear for his life. He turned away and, with his fiddle under his arm, slowly climbed the stairs to his room. Jake Holl stood at the bottom of the staircase and waited for the little man to return with his gold.

But the fiddler failed to return. Instead, the air was suddenly filled with the sound of a violin being played with the skill of a virtuoso, echoing through the house with a melody of such beauty as had never before been heard within those walls. Jake Holl, however, was not impressed and, picking up a knife, he bounded up the stairs and burst into the fiddler's room. The music stopped and there was just one more sound – a kind of slumping noise rather like that of a body falling on the floor. Then there was silence until Jake Holl, his face contorted with rage, reappeared and, almost tumbling down the stairs, fled through his front door and disappeared into the dark of the night. Neither he nor Old Tom were ever seen again.

The lodging house stayed closed, for the story of the night's happenings spread quickly and, knowing its guilty secret, the local folk deemed it prudent to leave the place alone. Occasionally, a prospective tenant, not knowing its history, would call to inspect the building, but such visits were always brief and, furthermore, each visitor would emerge with ashen face and a strange tale to tell. In the little room where the fiddler had lodged there was a little wooden chair and, on the floor beside it, a mysterious stain. As the visitor looked at the stain and pondered upon its origin, a phosphorescent glow would arise from the floor and gradually become transformed into the figure of Old Tom, playing his fiddle with all the flowing ease of a master musician.

Jake Holl's lodging house never opened its doors again, and the demolition which Hitler's Air Force started in 1942 was finally completed by developers in 1969. Black Horse Row has faded into history, taking with it the secret of that fateful Christmas Eve.

When it came to building up a knowledge of the rows, my cousin had a distinct advantage over me, for he lived in the town and, in his boyhood days, walked them all. The only ones I knew were those which drew me to them for some special purpose, and thus the majority were completely unknown territory. When I was about sixteen, however, there was one which I was determined to visit, for it had been the birthplace of one of my boyhood idols who had recently died. Thus it was that I went on a kind of pilgrimage to Row 36, otherwise known as Garden Row, for it was there, at No. 8, that Arthur Henry Patterson was born.

Arthur Patterson was the little boy who, from humble beginnings, became one of the most highly acclaimed naturalists of his day and who, under his pseudonym of "John Knowlittle", delighted readers of his many books and other publications. In my early years, much of my knowledge of natural history was acquired from cigarette cards but, every week in our local paper, John Knowlittle's notes appeared and they were all carefully filed away in a cardboard box in my bedroom cupboard. At first I was unaware that it was not his true identity and, when the truth became known to me, I felt it to be a singularly inappropriate name for a man who obviously knew so much. Perhaps the reason for his choice of nom-de-plume is best explained in his own words: "I prefer to dabble in every nature puddle, as far as my own East Coast corner is concerned. I saw plainly that I should not know too much in the great field; I could hope to *know* but *little,* hence my coupling of the two words".

Arthur Patterson was the youngest of eight children of a shoemaker, but he never knew most of his brothers and sisters, for he was the only one to survive past the age of 21. To make matters worse, his mother died when he was barely three and then, in the words of Beryl Tooley in her admirable biography of her great grandfather, "in her place came a stepmother – a devout Primitive unused to little boys who brought home newts and water snails, silkworms, bumble bees, rats, white mice and hedgehogs".

He seems always to have been plagued with money problems and, in his early married life, he became successively a relief postman, a pedlar of tea, a ticket collector at the Aquarium Theatre and a keeper at Preston Zoo. It was not until he was 35, when he was appointed School Attendance Officer, that he began to earn a regular living wage. Each day he would be out and about, armed with the long cane which became his trade mark, rounding up truant boys from places like the fishwharf and the railway tracks. Many a battle of wits took place between the boys and the man they called "Old Arthur", in most of which it was Old Arthur who was the winner. By the time he retired, after 35 years as Truant Officer, he was a highly respected figure and the children acknowledged this fact by referring to him more courteously as "Mr. Patt'son".

All his life he kept diaries and notebooks and he wrote whenever he could. Indeed, during the course of his lifetime he wrote 26 books and numerous pamphlets and articles for a variety of periodicals. Sadly for him, it was not a time when a living could be made from being a naturalist and, indeed, he lost money on the publication of his writings. It is somewhat ironic that his books are now eagerly sought after by dealers and collectors at highly inflated prices.

Though he ranged far and wide, there can be no doubt that his favourite haunt was Breydon Water, that vast estuary of the River Yare which inspired so much of his writing. There, on those four and a half miles of tidal mudflats, he met that strange race of eel-catchers and wildfowlers, the Breydoners. Indeed, he did not just meet them – he became one of them for, though by nature reticent almost to the point of distrust, they somehow accepted this stranger in their midst with barely a question. It is doubtful whether anyone else could have done it and thereby tell the story of those hardy, illiterate, self-contained watermen.

"They looked upon me as a camp follower and somewhat of an enigma", he said. "I pocketed a notebook and filled the pages with Breydon lore and anecdotes, gleaning up what to them was commonplace".

The cost of paper must have dug deeply into Arthur Patterson's financial resources for, quite apart from his diaries and notebooks, he was an inveterate letter-writer. He never failed to reply to the many people who wrote to him, and for many of them he provided a delightfully individual touch in the form of an illustrated envelope. His pen and ink sketches of water birds, which he could dash off in a matter of seconds, were well-known, and the illustrations which he applied to his letter covers were an extension of these. Each was individual and appropriate to the recipient, and I am grateful to Diana Rollason for allowing me to reproduce one of those received by her father in 1923. He was Richard Lipscomb, a dental practitioner in Desborough and later, for many years, in Fakenham, and he had much in common with Patterson. He was a countryman at heart, with a great understanding of the natural world, and he, too, was a regular contributor to various publications, notably the "Fishing Gazette"

To J.G. Jaane Esq
Desborough
Market Harborough

1ᴰ
511

Turnstone "No Fee!"

and the "Shooting Times". He wrote under the pseudonym of J.G. Jaane (dentists were not allowed to advertise themselves in any way) and it was by that name that Patterson knew him.

I met Arthur Patterson just once, when I was eleven years old and he was already in his mid-seventies. It was a chance meeting, for I had gone to the "Eastern Daily Press" office in Yarmouth, where the manager at the time was Harry Hurrell, and this elderly man with the grey moustache and goatee beard came through the doorway. The two men had much in common, for Mr. Hurrell was also a naturalist, with a particular interest in the minute aquatic life of Breydon and the Broads. Indeed, they were both officers of Yarmouth Naturalists' Society, Hurrell being Chairman and Patterson vice-chairman. It so happens that one of the joint secretaries at that time was a young man named Edward A. Ellis – the same Ted Ellis who, in later years, was destined to bring

Arthur Patterson with Harry Hurrell at Yarmouth Press Office, 1931.

Dictating "Wildfowlers and Poachers" to the youthful Ted Ellis.

pleasure and enlightenment to millions as Norfolk's great man of Nature. His family had recently come to Gorleston from Guernsey, and he and Patterson immediately recognised their common bond. They spent much time in each other's company and it was Ted, in fact, who typed the manuscript of "Wildfowlers and Poachers" when Patterson prepared it for publication in 1929.

One cannot help thinking that, in the young Ted Ellis, Patterson found some kind of replacement for his own naturalist son, Gerald, whose death on the Somme in 1916 had left him heartbroken. The bond between the older man and his protegé became very strong, and it was Patterson who urged Ted to apply for the post of naturalist at the Castle Museum in Norwich in November 1928. In later years, Ted Ellis was ever ready to acknowledge the great influence that Patterson had on his life.

When Arthur Henry Patterson died in 1935 he left behind him both an inspiration and an example to those who followed him. He had never known affluence but there is one redeeming thought for, as Beryl Tooley says in her biography: " . . . he was fortunate to have lived at a time when Broadland was a wildlife paradise. His old heart would grieve today for his beloved Breydon and to see how Broadland has changed".

CHAPTER 14

Holidays and History.

One of the thrills of my early visits to Yarmouth was a ride on the Scenic Railway. It was 1932 and that great construction, claimed to be the biggest switchback in Europe, had just been installed. It was a somewhat frightening experience, only partly relieved by the artistic layout which transformed it into a journey through a vast range of snow-capped mountains. I have never had much of a yearning for thrills of that nature, but taking a ride on that great monster was a necessity of boyhood. To have declined would have led to a certain loss of face with one's contemporaries, together with accusations of being a "cissy".

The first thing to catch one's eye on coming to the end of the ride was a large notice offering those of us who were willing to stay in our seats a repeat trip around the course at half price. I never availed myself of that bargain offer. I was more intent on getting my feet onto a firm base and allowing my internal organs to sort themselves out and regain some semblance of normality. But the Scenic Railway, and the funfair which went with it, was just a part of the brash, artificial image which the town had steadily developed in its effort to become one of Britain's major seaside resorts.

When the medical profession had first proclaimed the virtues of salt water and sea air, Yarmouth had reacted in the same way as Cromer and many other resorts. Up went the bath houses and reading rooms where visitors could scan the pages of the London newspapers. Down on the beach came the little white bell tents and rows of bathing machines, together with a myriad of other attractions. There was the camera obscura, rather like a very early form of live television, which threw a living picture of the entire beach scene through a lens and on to a large white screen. Today's holiday-makers would probably regard this as an intrusion into their personal privacy, but it was said to be extremely useful to mothers searching for lost children! There was Madame Cook, the renowned phrenologist, who could foretell your prospects by "reading your bumps", and there were the beach concert parties, notably Chappell's Promenade Concert with its ever-popular performing poodles.

Gorleston Beach in 1904.

There were, of course, rides for everybody. Down on the shore, the fishermen overloaded their rowing boats and sailing yawls with visitors anxious for a trip on the briny. Up on the promenade, four-horse brakes took their passengers for rides in the country until they themselves were driven from the streets by the advent of the motor charabanc. One of the men who witnessed this transformation was my great-uncle, William Worton, who, in 1910, was advertising himself as "Post Master and Cab Proprietor, Dog Carts and Waggonettes, General Carting &c." Before many years had passed, his "Norfolk Stables" in St. George's Road had become a "Motor Garage" and he had acquired a fleet of Armstrong Siddeleys which were a source of great interest to Classic Car enthusiasts. Meanwhile, the children were not forgotten. For them there were the donkeys and the quaint little goat carts whilst, on the forecourt of the Hippodrome, there was the much-loved pony with its cart built in the shape of a miniature lifeboat.

But Yarmouth was not content to leave it at that. Unlike some resorts, she was not willing to await natural development. Up went the hotels and boarding houses, together with every possible form

The garage where my great-uncle changed from one type of horse power to another.

The lifeboat-shaped pony cart outside the Hippodrome.

of amusement which man could devise. It was, of course, the railways which brought most holidaymakers to the town, but many Londoners came by sea. At Tower Bridge they would board the little fleet of Belle Steamers, so called because they all bore such names as Southend Belle or Yarmouth Belle, and, at a cost of ten shillings, they would make their way up the coast, calling at other resorts on the way. Some of them looked distinctly green when they came down the gangway at Yarmouth, to be met by cab-drivers and landladies touting for business. Many of them, however, were already spoken for, for they were the notorious Garibaldi Boys.

It was Joe Powell, the proprietor of the Garibaldi Hotel, who organised the annual invasions by hundreds of young London men, most of whom spent their working lives as clerks in City Offices and counting houses. They were a high-spirited crowd and did not always live up to his description of them as the Garibaldi Gents or, more informally, his "Lambs". They came to "Bloaterland" determined to have a good time, and this sometimes led them into such activities as invading the stage during Concert Party performances or disturbing the privacy of courting couples who would have preferred to have been left alone. There were occasions when, having sinned against the accepted standards of behaviour, their week in Yarmouth included an appearance before the local magistrates. This did not endear either them or the "Gari" to some of the local populace but, for the most part, their misdemeanours were little more than harmless larking about. Indeed, they usually redeemed themselves by finding ways of raising money for various charities during their stay in the town.

Whether one loves or loathes the holiday aspect of Great Yarmouth, there is no denying the fact that it has always had much to offer its visitors. It is difficult, for instance, to imagine the sea-front without its two piers. It was the Wellington which came first, though it has seen many additions and alterations since 1853 in an effort to keep up with the ever-changing demands of visitors. I remember it best in the days when the Pavilion played host to such performers as Leslie Henson and the Tatlers Concert Party, when the spacious Gardens echoed to the sound of light music emanating from the ornate bandstand, and when the Winter Garden, with its palm trees and potted ferns, was the mecca for roller skating enthusiasts and devotees of the tea dance. But times have changed and the Wellington has changed with them.

The Belle Steamers arriving from London.

The Garibaldi Boys in residence.

The Wellington Gardens.

The Aquarium and Revolving Tower.

145

The Britannia Pier arrived in 1858 and there are many who would claim that it has long been, and still remains, Yarmouth's greatest asset. To say that the Britannia has had a chequered career would be something of an understatement, for twice it has been cut in two by ships and at least four times it has been ravaged by fire. One of the earlier fires, in 1914, is believed to have been started by suffragettes, but probably the worst such disaster was that which, in 1954, destroyed the Ocean Ballroom and restaurant and the 1,230 seat Pavilion Theatre, together with children's rides, amusements and the coastguard lookout. Once again it was rebuilt, though not in its original form. Whereas all the previous pavilions had presented a distinctly oriental appearance, with domes and pinnacles, the new one had such a functional design that it soon received the nickname of "the aircraft hangar".

Not far from the Britannia Pier the skyline was dominated for many years by the Revolving Tower, a 100-foot structure which offered wonderful views of the landscape all around. As its name implies, the cage which took the passengers up and down revolved as it did so, thus providing views for many miles in all directions. A good indication of how times change is given by the fact that, as I write these lines, Great Yarmouth has just acquired its latest tourist attraction in the form of a drilling platform called Penrod 80. Standing 343 feet tall, it would certainly have dwarfed the hundred feet of the Revolving Tower, but it seems that Penrod 80 does nothing but stand there waiting to be looked at. The older structure did at least do something – or perhaps I should say it normally did something, for it was inclined to be slightly unreliable. Breakdowns were not uncommon and, at such times, passengers would be marooned until workmen carried out repairs. There was an emergency ladder down which they could climb, but a hundred feet is a long way and most of them preferred to wait. There is one recorded case of a lady who, having a pressing engagement, decided to climb down the ladder, but she refused to do so unless a man would climb up and hold down her skirts and petticoats to protect her modesty as she descended. Happily, a volunteer was found and both safely negotiated the ladder with no sign of offence to public morals. (Since writing the above lines, Penrod 80 has departed from the Yarmouth scene. Its degree of success as a magnet for visitors is difficult to evaluate but, at least, it was unique both in its size and in the brevity of its stay).

There were so many other attractions in those carefree boyhood days between the wars that to list them all would be impossible. There was, for instance, the Hippodrome, which was always full of surprises. I confess that, for me, the circus performances had only limited appeal, but there was always a surge of excitement when the floor suddenly sank to reveal a watery arena in which the rest of the entertainment took place. There was the open-air swimming pool which later gave way to the Marina, with its memories of concert parties, bathing beauty contests and Neville Bishop and his Band. And, of course, there was the Pleasure Beach in its quieter days before the surge into the age of blaring pop music and thrill-a-minute roller-coaster rides. The Scenic Railway was bearable, there were slot machines in which one could invest as little as a penny (or even a ha'penny) and still stand a chance of winning as much as threepence – and there was Professor Powley, who would climb a ladder to a high platform, set himself on fire and then dive, with his clothes all alight, into a small tank of water, which extinguished the flames.

But I suppose the biggest change of all is to be found on the South Denes. There, in earlier times, fishermen had spread their nets to dry and local people had common grazing rights. The early militia trained there, and it was even the site of a racecourse before the new one was laid out in 1922. In the days of my boyhood it was the wide open space where children played and flew kites, where visitors camped and had picnics, and where, in the fishing season, thousands of barrels were stacked to await the harvest of the sea. And, of course, it was the place from which Britannia, perched on top of the Nelson Monument, looked across the county towards the Admiral's birthplace at Burnham Thorpe.

Nowadays, Britannia has to crane her neck to even catch a glimpse of the sky, for Yarmouth has been industrialised and the Denes have been caught up in this new era. Even the cranes which built the power station looked down upon her, and now she is surrounded by food packing plants and factories as the town has made the switch from fishing to shore-based industries.

What an extraordinary jumble of a place Yarmouth has become! The summer visitors make their pleasure-seeking pilgrimage and focus their attentions on the Front, which is so full of enticing amusements that very few of them ever see the beach. The men of industry spend their time in anonymous buildings in equally anonymous roads in an effort to meet the ever-increasing demands

The open-air Marina Theatre.

Neville Bishop comperes the weekly bathing beauty contest.

148

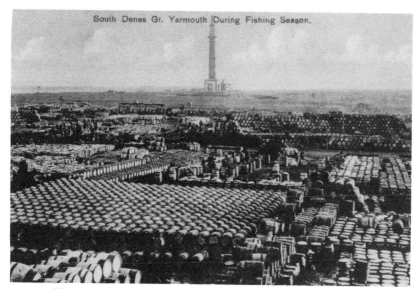

Herring barrels stacked on the South Denes during the fishing season.

The Market Place and the Penny Bazaar.

of our present-day consumer society. In between stand the early Victorian squares of grey brick houses which, though they now look out upon a much-changed world, still somehow manage to cling to a simple element of grace to remind us of Yarmouth's genteel beginnings as a health resort. But then, of course, there is the old town where it all began and where, in spite of devastation in two World Wars, Yarmouth still retains its heart and its true character.

In common with many other old ports, which valued the sea for purposes of trade rather than as a leisure facility, the old town ignored the coastline and grew up around the harbour and the market. The favoured outlook of the merchants was on the source of their wealth and, while most of the population were packed like sardines in the narrow confines of the Rows, the finest houses were built facing the busy quays and the wide sweep of the Market Place. In the days of my boyhood the market was a fascination, for it had an atmosphere which I have never found anywhere else. It was a place where, so we were told, you could buy such delicacies as cow's udder, cow heel, tripe and huge Portuguese oysters at a shilling apiece. That may well have been true, but I preferred to confine my attentions to such familiar favourites as cockles and whelks. In more recent years the Market Place has had to battle against the ever-increasing demands of the motor car, but in those earlier times it was part of the very history of the town.

It was in my early youth that I first became aware that, far from being merely a place for holidays and herring fishing, Yarmouth was steeped in history. It all started when I attended a wedding reception in the old Star Hotel, that fine building which has faced out onto Hall Quay for something like four hundred years. Indeed, it was not long before I found myself showing greater interest in the building itself than in the celebrations which were going on around me. It was built, I was told, by a certain William Crowe who had become a successful man of business and had been appointed bailiff of Yarmouth. He had obviously spared no expense in the erection of his sumptuous home, for the whole place was elaborate in the extreme. It was the so-called Nelson Room on the upper floor, however, that most captured my imagination with its grandly decorated ceiling and finely carved wall panelling. It was said that Nelson had slept in that room during one of his visits to the town, but whether or not there is truth in that claim I cannot say.

What cannot be denied, however, is that he did come ashore at Yarmouth on November 6th 1800 after he had fought and won the Battle of the Nile, and that day was a momentous one in the town's history. The enthusiastic townsfolk turned out in strength and, removing the horses from his carriage, pulled him through the crowded streets to the old Wrestlers' Hotel, where he received the freedom of the borough. It was during the ceremony that Nelson laid his left hand on the book as the Town Clerk prepared to administer the oath, causing that local worthy to admonish him with: "Your *right* hand if you please, my lord". "That", replied Nelson, "is at Teneriffe", at which the civic fathers once again shouted themselves hoarse in admiration. Later in the day the Admiral, accompanied by Sir William and Lady Hamilton and a vast congregation, went to the church of St. Nicholas to give thanks to God for the success of the British fleet. After that eventful day there can hardly have been any town in the country where Nelson's activities were watched with greater interest than at Yarmouth, and it is little wonder that, after the victory at Trafalgar which cost him his life, the monument to his memory should have arisen on the South Denes.

It seems strange that, in spite of its long history, Yarmouth has had comparatively few sons and daughters who have achieved lasting fame. There was Admiral Perebrowne, the first Admiral of the Nore, and Sir John Fastolf, who built Caister Castle and became one of the greatest soldiers of his day. In the world of literature there was Anna Sewell, the creator of "Black Beauty", and "John Knowlittle", the eminent Broadland naturalist, but in most other cases it has been a question of association rather than birth. Daniel Defoe was a frequent, and admiring, visitor to the area, and it was in a storm which blew up just off the port that the adventures of Robinson Crusoe began. But most of all there was Charles Dickens and David Copperfield who have become so much a part of Yarmouth's history that some of us can never think of one without the other.

It is said that the author acquired much of the background material for his book from Jack Sharman, an old veteran of Trafalgar, who was the keeper of the Nelson Monument. He also had much first-hand knowledge of the area, and it was he who said, "If you bear a grudge against any particular insurance office, purchase from it a heavy life annuity, go live at Yarmouth and draw your dividends until they ask you in despair whether your name be

Peggotty's Hut as seen by a film producer. This was, in fact, erected on the beach at Benacre for a film of "David Copperfield" which featured Sir Laurence Olivier, Sir Michael Redgrave, Sir Ralph Richardson, Sir Richard Attenborough and Dame Edith Evans, 1971.

Old Parr or Methuselah". The town took great pride in the association and I recall, in my boyhood, seeing quite a selection of structures, some being upturned boats with chimneys and others more conventional upright buildings, which all proclaimed themselves as being "Peggotty's Hut".

It was in the old town that all Yarmouth's historic associations were built up and it is there that, for me, the town's heart still beats as it has done for centuries. Even now, when I visit the place, it is only rarely that I make straight for the Front. Much nicer, I feel, to exercise the privilege of a friend and go in by the back door.

CHAPTER 15

City Streets.

Every man has his first love and, as far as the thoroughfares of Norwich are concerned, it was Prince of Wales Road which first captured my heart. Admittedly, my emotions were greatly influenced by the fact that it was that road which, when I was six years old, gave me my first glimpse of the city in which I was later to live for many years. But it was a stately road in those days and it always seemed to extend a welcoming hand as we arrived on the North Walsham train and proceeded to deal with whatever matter of business had brought us to the city.

Those early day trips were by no means frequent and were dictated solely by the needs of one or other of my parents. When I accompanied my mother we usually engaged in a round of visits to relatives scattered around the city but, with my father, our attentions were focussed mainly on the Press Office and the Fish Market. Of course, I was unaware at that time that Prince of Wales Road was the baby of the city's family of thoroughfares, having been created specifically to serve the needs of the new railway some eighty years earlier. To me it was simply the bustling, prosperous avenue which opened the curtain on the wonders of the big city.

It was a symbol of early Victorian Norwich, sweeping away in a gentle curve up to the splendid private houses at the top, where lived the doctors, lawyers and other members of the professional classes. Even the licensed houses had been caught up in the appealing pretentiousness of the period, calling themselves after the Prince of Wales, the Duke of Connaught and the Duke of Beaufort. And, of course, there were trees everywhere – the Victorians loved their trees.

On my early visits to Norwich it was the relentless hustle and bustle on that spacious road which held me in its spell for, even then, it was a different world from the one in which we lived. There were handcarts and horse-drawn delivery wagons; there were pedestrians and cyclists, and women pushing prams; there was even the occasional motor car. But, above all, there were the trams. I readily confess to a great affection for the old trams and I still regret that they have now become nothing more than a symbol of the past. It is true that they provided little comfort and indeed, if one travelled on the top deck after a shower of rain, the wet seats made it advisable to make the journey in a standing position. Yet we were content to rumble and crash along, facing each other on slatted wooden benches, at a mere ten or twelve miles an hour. Then, on the more open stretches, we would pitch and roll as the iron wheels crashed in the tracks and sparks flew from the overhead wires. It was then that the tram made it clear that it was putting everything it had into its task, as also did the driver who, with his red nose and walrus moustache, looked for all the world as though he had stepped straight off one of the old horse omnibuses.

Throughout the length of Prince of Wales Road there are places which still evoke memories of those early boyhood years. There was the big store where C.W. Willmott proclaimed the wonders of the wide range of wireless sets which he had for sale and where, also, my mother parted with the sum of three pounds fifteen shillings to buy my first bicycle. Standing opposite were the two cinemas, the Regent and the Electric (later called the Norvic) where I was destined to spend many a happy hour. And there was Maudes of Norwich who offered to supply any make of car and where patrons of the Electric Cinema were offered free parking – but only those who sat in the 1/-, 1/3d and 1/6d seats. Presumably those who frequented the cheaper seats arrived by tram!

It is at the very top of the road, however, that the memories crowd in thick and fast, for it was there that so much happened in the days when Norwich was part country town and only part industrial city. Before it was moved to Harford Bridges in 1960, the Cattle Market had been held in the shadow of the Castle for at least three centuries and Saturday was the day when the country came to town. Every week the sights and sounds (not to mention the smells) of the farmyard transformed the area where commuters now park their motor cars. It was all rather inconvenient at times, for much of the livestock was herded through the streets from all directions. The route from City Station along Barn Road and St. Benedict's was particularly busy, with startled housewives suddenly finding themselves joined at the counter of a shop by a stray cow. Even the trams, which normally controlled the speed of the traffic flow, found it necessary to give precedence to the four-legged country visitors, and I also recall the sight of two

My first glimpse of Prince of Wales Road.

Further along, showing the Electric Cinema.

The Cattle Market in the shadow of the Castle.

Even the trams had to give way to the weekly country visitors.

frustrated men endeavouring to escort a herd of reluctant pigs across the wide expanse of All Saints' Green. But the people of Norwich accepted it all, for it was the one day of the week when they were happy to acknowledge their agricultural roots.

In association with the market there was the Agricultural Hall, built in 1882 and now forming part of the Anglia Television complex. To the farming community it was the centre for such occasions as the Spring Stallion Show and, in October, a similar event for Fat Cattle, but to the people of the city it rapidly became the focal point of a wide range of activities. Every year, the men of the 20th Hussars would start things off with a military tournament in aid of local medical charities, and then the circus would move in. Hengler's Circus was probably most notable for introducing to Norwich Whimsical Walker, one of the greatest of clowns, with his red hot poker and his succession of performing cats, dogs and donkeys.

It was George Gilbert, however, who really drew the crowds, to such an extent that his season lasted for three months. He and his wife, Jenny O'Brien, were renowned bareback riders, but the main reason for his success was the continuous variety which he brought into the programme. I never personally witnessed the performance, but I heard so much about it in my childhood days that I can almost imagine I had been there. There were Colibri's Midgets, Judge's Cockatoos and Lockhart's Elephants, to say nothing of the Greco-Roman wrestlers who packed the hall two years in succession with their bouts between the Terrible Turks and the Grim Greeks! Then, most memorable of all, there was the occasion when Blondin appeared and carried a man across a tightrope suspended above the audience. To our grandparents it was a never-to-be-forgotten experience.

When not in use for some such large event, the Agricultural Hall was a popular venue for roller skating, although the fact that the floor consisted of somewhat uneven wooden blocks tended to make it a slightly uncomfortable experience. One would have thought there was little need for the large notice saying "ALL SKATE SLOWLY" which was prominently displayed. The price of admission was one shilling, which included use of skates and instruction for beginners, and there was continuous musical accompaniment. Furthermore, in the words of the proprietor, Mr. W.G. Becker, the establishment was "Patronised by the Elite".

Roller skating in the Agricultural Hall.

Among the host of activities which have taken place in the Agricultural Hall there can be little doubt that the Ideal Homes Exhibition is the one which is best remembered. The Hall was packed from floor to gallery with everything which could conceivably be connected with the average home, plus much more besides. The centrepiece of the whole affair was a massive fountain which, illuminated by coloured lights from the ceiling, threw cascades of water into the air, to the accompaniment of a string orchestra playing "Nights of Gladness" and a popular tune of the day entitled "Home". On one occasion, Boulton and Paul's erected a bungalow which, complete with verandah, was on offer for the sum of £100. At the same time, Geo. Tyce (House Furnishers) were advertising their willingness to completely furnish four rooms, even with such details as a coal scuttle and glass vase, for £40.

Many local manufacturers and suppliers were there, not least being Coleman's, who had achieved fame with their Wincarnis Tonic Wine. At one time Mr. Coleman had attempted to repeat the success with his new tonic Cocoa, but somehow it failed to capture the public's imagination. He thus turned to Old English Wine Jelly made, we were told, with the flavour of black wine grapes. "Invalids can't resist it – children love it" was the claim, which seems reasonable, for jelly has always been the one thing which any normal invalid is expected to be capable of eating. The great new product for the exhibition, however, was Odol Tooth Paste, which certainly did achieve a fair degree of success. Furthermore, advertisements informed us that it was personally praised by such screen and stage stars as Betty Balfour, Winifred Shotter, Janet Gaynor, Laura La Plante and Richard Tauber. As an added attraction, a famous film star was to appear on the Odol stand at the Exhibition. She duly arrived and Clifford Temple, that inveterate snapshotter, took a photo of her. Sadly, however, none of us had ever heard of her.

In spite of that disappointment it was a wonderful day out, with many memories to savour. There was the joy of sitting at little tables and drinking free cups of cocoa, the thrill of visiting every stand and endeavouring to scrounge free samples of the products, and then staggering home with a heavy load of leaflets and brochures which eventually found their way into the dustbin.

Twice a year, however, both the Cattle Market and the Agricultural Hall were cleared to make way for one of the greatest thrills of our boyhood years – the Fair. At Easter and Christmas the showmen would arrive and, in seemingly no time at all, both Hall and Market would be packed with every conceivable kind of diversion, with hardly an inch to spare anywhere. It was still the traditional type of gathering, with the hissing of steam from the traction engines, the tooting of whistles, the heat of the paraffin flares and the ornate old organs with figures beating on drums and crashing cymbals to fill the air with mechanical music.

There were the Galloping Horses, Thurston's Dragons and the Cake Walk. There were the renowned Swinging Boats, Shamrock and Resolute, taking their names from the yachts which competed for the Americas Cup in the days when Sir Thomas Lipton carried the British flag to victory. And there was Billy Wood's International Boxing Academy where foolhardy local lads risked life and limb in an effort to overcome the travelling pugilists. On a more modest scale, there was an absolute plethora of hoop-la stalls, coconut shies and shooting galleries, not to mention the stalls offering fairground rock in a wide selection of flavours and colours.

The greatest variety, however, was to be found in the many booths which housed attractions as diverse as knife-throwing acts and flea circuses. Many offered a selection of animal exhibits, from

Helter Skelters at the Fair.

Tianga, the Jungle Girl.

the Biggest Rat in the World (which turned out to be a coypu) to a selection of freaks of nature – I recall a five-legged sheep, although I never actually saw it. In most cases, however, the animals on show were accompanied by young ladies who, in the context of the period, were regarded as being somewhat scantily clad. Who, indeed, can forget Rona the Rat Girl, sharing a cage with crawling rodents, or Tianga the Jungle Girl, who held up such things as lizards for close inspection by her audience?

They were, indeed, heady days and, even when the main attractions departed for pastures new, a selection of rides and stalls remained in the Agricultural Hall to give continued delight to the younger generation.

As I have intimated, the character of my early visits to Norwich differed according to which of my parents was escorting me. With my mother, formality was the keynote, the highlight being a tram ride to Essex Street for lunch with my grandmother. The meal itself was something of a ritual, with a dish of dumplings to be consumed before we reached the main part of the meal. With my father, however, things could hardly have been more different and I am not at all sure that my mother would have approved of the manner in which he initiated me into one of the joys of adulthood, for we took our meal at the cockle stall on the corner of the Market Place. The cockles were served on little dishes priced at a halfpenny each, for which sum one could also have a couple of whelks or a thick hunk of bread. The really exciting part, however, was learning for the first time how adults dealt with the tasty shellfish, for it was all done in accordance with a time-honoured tradition. Having selected one's dish, one sprinkled the cockles with pepper and then liberally soaked them in vinegar. Then, having spread one's fingers over the cockles and tucked one's thumb underneath the dish, one inverted the whole thing and shook the surplus vinegar into the gutter. Only then could the meal begin. It was all tremendously exciting, and the memory of that early initiation into manhood is something which has stayed with me over the years. Even more notable was the fact that no payment was made until we had finished our meal, when the stallkeeper counted the empty dishes and charged my father accordingly. It was the first time I had ever eaten anything without first paying for it. It was, indeed, one of the greatest landmarks in my life.

The rest of the market was full of fascination, though nothing quite equalled the magic of the cockle stall. My memory tells me that there were more stalls in my boyhood days, but I know that to be false for they were not set out in the orderly rows of the present day. Indeed, they looked almost as though somebody had dropped them at random from above. It was always a very bustling place and there must have been times when the poor old Duke of Wellington, looking out onto Gentleman's Walk from his vantage point between the tram shelter and the public conveniences, must have felt distinctly hemmed in. No doubt he has been happier since 1937 when they took him to stand back-to-back with Lord Nelson in the Cathedral Close.

The busiest time of all on the Market Place was on Saturday evenings, for it was the custom for all the stalls to be dismantled and taken away for the week-end, and traders thus had the habit of reducing their prices as the day wore on in order to dispose of as much stock as possible. This practice certainly drew the crowds and the phrase, "like the back of the market on a Saturday night", became the traditional way of describing any scene of great activity. Sunday left the old municipal buildings (which, incidentally, now seem too fine to have been demolished back in the thirties) gazing down on the wide open spaces of the market square. For one day in the week all was still – until anybody who felt so inclined could address an audience by climbing on a cart and giving forth. This was a common practice at election time, and heckling became something of a fine art in which voters soon discovered the worth of prospective candidates.

One of the many trams which passed by the Market Place travelled the full length of St. Giles' Street where, in my teenage years, the bookshops became a happy hunting ground. Indeed, riding on the top of a tram as it swung round almost at right angles from St. Giles' Gates into Unthank Road was an exhilarating experience, especially on frosty mornings when the wheels had a tendency to leave the rails. St. Giles' Gates, where many an early convict met his grisly fate, was part of a five-way junction receiving all the traffic from the south-west of the city along both Earlham Road and Unthank Road. Now things have changed and the St. Giles' Gates Stores and the chemist's shop no longer face each

The Duke of Wellington looks out over the Market Place.

The jumble of the Market before the background buildings were demolished.

An old tram passes St. Giles' Gates on its way from Magdalen Road to Unthank Road.

Another passes Barn Road on the way from the Royal Hotel to Dereham Road.

other across that busy street. Instead, further down, the ancient church stands sentinel over the divided halves of the street, with the lower half struggling manfully to cope with an inflow of traffic for which it was never designed whilst the upper part has been blessed with a certain air of serenity. Meanwhile, the one thing that never changes is the row of wisterias which regularly hang their blossoms around the edge of the churchyard, just as they did all those years ago.

The streets of Norwich, transformed though they may be, still cry out with memories for, in my boyhood, I explored them all with the thoroughness of an architectural historian. Busy streets and narrow alleys, courtyards and lanes all came within my compass and, linking them all together, there were the trams. There was a sense of solidarity about the trams, for they had a restraining influence on scurrying motor cars and they promoted a sense of moderation in the speed of our progress. But I suppose they were never really successful. There had been much opposition to their introduction, with shopkeepers and the residential gentry protesting that they were being deprived of their ancient right to have van or carriage standing outside their door. There had been strong protests about the extent of the demolitions needed to enable them to negotiate the narrow streets and abrupt corners. Then there was the suspected element of danger to pedestrians, and I recall a childhood jingle which must surely have been promoted by the anti-tram faction. I hope I quote it correctly after all these years:

> "Oh, Mother dear, what have we here?
> It looks like strawberry jam!"
> "Hush, hush, my child, it's poor Papa,
> Run over by a tram".

The trams won the battle, but it was something of a hollow victory. They clanged their way through the city for some thirty-five uneasy years until the more manoeuvrable motor buses drove them from the streets.

But somehow, even now, Prince of Wales Road doesn't look quite right without its trams.

CHAPTER 16

Characters of Old Norwich.

It is my sincere belief that no account of the city's earlier personalities would be complete without a mention of Grandma Bagshaw. In saying this, however, I have to admit to a certain amount of bias, for I suppose the dear lady never did anything of sufficient import to endear her memory to any but her immediate circle of friends and relatives. Nevertheless, to me she was the very epitome of everything that was best in the era of Victorianism to which she belonged.

A busy little dumpling of a lady, she had a permanent twinkle in her eye, which refused to be dimmed even when she was issuing a reprimand concerning something which displeased her. Such occasions, anyway, were rare, and the worst I ever received was when, having been engaged in street games with other local lads, I arrived on her doorstep to be greeted with, "Oh, deary me! What a state you're in! Pull them socks up and let me run a comb through your hair. You look a proper little shuck." Then she would usher me through to her back parlour, sit me down at the little table and put before me the latest delicacy to emerge from her oven in the wall.

Sadly, she had lost her husband even before I was born, but life went on the way it had always been when he had been conducting his affairs in the business life of the city. His photograph gazed down from the parlour wall and she continued to rule over the little empire of modest houses which he had built up in the area around their Essex Street home. Regularly she did her rounds to collect the odd shillings in rent and to ensure the well-being of her tenants, then returning to Number Thirty with the satisfied air of a midwife after another safe delivery.

It was our conversations in that little back parlour, however, which stand out in my memory – how sad that tape recorders had not been invented! She regaled me with a multitude of tales of earlier times, all the while bending over her ironing or dashing backwards and forwards creating tempting aromas in that little wall-oven. Her memories seemed never-ending as she recalled a bygone age and the people who lived in it – and it was the people who most fascinated me. People, for instance, like Childerhouse, the Bellman.

In purely physical terms, William Childerhouse was a somewhat insignificant little man; indeed, the only part of him which made any impact on the casual observer was the majestic pair of mutton chop whiskers on which he lavished such care and attention. But Childerhouse had other attributes which were destined to make him one of the best-known figures in Norwich at the turn of the century. To begin with, there was his bubbling personality, together with the fact that he did everything in life at top speed. Above all, however, there was his voice. Described as a deep bass, it was of such volume that he could be heard over a vast area as he advertised his wares. Indeed, the reaction of most people on encountering it for the first time was rather akin to that of somebody listening to the song of a wren – it was amazing that such a tiny throat could produce so great a volume of sound.

In the early 1870's Childerhouse divided his time between the little shop in Alexandra Road, where he dispensed the somewhat unlikely combination of mussels and watercress, and the local Baptist chapel where he was a preacher. It was then, however, that Fate took a hand in his life in the person of one James Spilling, who lived nearby. Mr. Spilling was the editor of the still-infant "Eastern Daily Press" and, wishing to boast the circulation of his paper, he decided that Childerhouse was the man for the job. Thus it was that the little man was put into a smart blue uniform with brass buttons and employed to hawk the paper around the city streets. Success was instantaneous and, before long, he had a company of a dozen or so newsboys working under his command. Almost overnight, the little man with the stentorian voice and the chirpy personality became a familiar figure throughout the city.

It was at this time that James Spilling wrote his book of Norfolk humour, "Giles's First Trip To London", in which he recounted the experiences of a typical Norfolk countryman (if there ever was such a being). The temptation to include Childerhouse in the narrative, even though not by name, proved too great and, at the point where he approaches Norwich, the mythical Giles declares:

> *"As we got near the city I heard a most 'mazing loud voice, afore I could see anybody, and that saamed to be telling the people all the news of the day. I say to myself, 'Ye'd du well to kaap the birds off the whate in our fifty-acre.' Presently I seed a little chap wi' gold letters on his hat, goin' along so quick*

that I thowt he must be on the Queen's sarvice, and he comes up to our waggon, and he say, 'Daily Press, gentlemen? Mornin' paaper, gentlemen? All the news o' the day! Only one penny'. 'Well,' I say to myself, 'He's a smart little chap. I'll have a punnorth o' him: it'll du to wrap suffin in if 'twon't du for northin' else.'"

Even then, greater fame lay ahead for Childerhouse when, in 1877, the City Fathers, seeking somebody to proclaim their official announcements, decided that the effervescent little fellow was just the man for the job. In any other town or city he would have become known as the Town Crier. Norwich, however, true to the Norfolk tradition of "doing different", proclaimed him "Childerhouse, The Bellman", a title which became perpetuated as part of the city's heritage. His salary for the appointment was 13s 4d per annum, hardly a princely sum and, furthermore, one which was never increased throughout his 28 years of service. Much more lucrative was his simultaneous appointment as sword bearer in the Corporation processions, for which he received five pounds a year, and there were other little extras for his services as toastmaster at civic banquets and the like. Above all, however, he had acquired professional status. Henceforth, organisers of concerts and sporting events, as well as local tradesmen, sought his help to publicise what they had to offer – all at a fee of half a crown for 40 "calls".

Thus, for the rest of his life, the little man trudged the streets of Norwich, with his ten-pound bell, every bit as big as his own head, held in the crook of his arm. Wherever he went he was among friends, and he was particularly acclaimed when, in the floods of 1878, he was dispatched to the affected areas to proclaim information concerning places where food and shelter could be obtained. At one point he lost his footing and fell into the raging torrent beneath but, almost within seconds, he emerged and climbed to safety, still smiling and still carrying his precious bell.

He remained in office until his death in 1905 at the age of 67 and there were many applicants when the corporation advertised for a successor. His was a hard act to follow, however, for there could be only one William Childerhouse. Eventually the choice was made and the post was given to Harry Moulton, who had previously played the big drum in the Salvation Army Band. He was a much more impressive figure than his predecessor and, with his neatly trimmed moustache and smart new uniform, he radiated an air of authority as he paraded around the city with his ever-present dog,

William Childerhouse.

Harry Moulton and Prince.

Prince. Sadly, however, he never seems to have evoked the degree of affection afforded to the little man who had gone before. Did he, as some people claimed, really lack the voice and personality of his predecessor, or could it have been that the people of Norwich, true to their native character, did not take kindly to the change in something they had loved for so long? Whatever the truth of the matter, the status of the appointment gradually faded and the post of Bellman was dropped.

In 1986, David Bullock appeared on the streets of Norwich in the guise of Town Crier. In these days of local radio and public address systems, however, such an appointment can surely be little more than an acknowledgement of the little man who played that role a hundred years earlier. In this technological age, even William Childerhouse wouldn't have stood a chance!

When I was about twelve years old, Grandma Bagshaw presented me with a postcard album bursting with pictures of actresses, singers and music hall performers – the pop stars of their day. She lovingly turned each page and told me all she knew about the faces which looked up at us. They were all there – Phyllis Dare and her sister Zena ("Two lovely ladies," said Grandma), Gertie Millar ("She played the part of Mary Gibbs in 'Our Miss Gibbs'," I was told), Florence Warde (holding her skirts above her knees in such a daring manner that Grandma quickly turned the page) and men such as Matheson Lang in costume for the part of Romeo. But the one over which she dwelt the longest was an opera singer. Portrayed by a drawing rather than an actual photograph, it was Jenny Lind, the Swedish Nightingale.

Grandma spoke of her at such great length and in such endearing terms that I began to think that they might, perhaps, have been friends. It therefore came as something of a surprise to learn that the dear lady had, in fact, been dead for nearly half a century. The high degree of reverence with which Grandma spoke of her, however, left me in no doubt that Jenny Lind was, indeed, somebody special. She was, I learned, a most beautiful lady and the loveliest singer in the world. She had been to Norwich several times, and Grandma knew people who had been to her concerts in St. Andrew's Hall. She was, also, not only a lady of the highest moral virtues but also very charitable, which is why we had a children's hospital which bore her name.

I decided to try to find out more about the Scandinavian opera singer and her connection with the Jenny Lind Hospital. It was some years before I managed to unravel the story, but when I had completed my task I had no difficulty in understanding why the earlier citizens of Norwich had held the name of Jenny Lind in such high esteem.

In 1847, when she made her first visit to England, she was at the peak of her career and, when it became known that she was to appear in Norwich, the people of the city readily succumbed to the fanatical surge of Jenny Lind fever which swept through the country. Her arrival in the city was, in fact, heralded by a joyous peal of the bells of St. Peter Mancroft, a tribute which, as far as I am aware, has never been accorded to any of the present generation of pop stars. There was, however, just one little cloud which threatened to cast a shadow over the great event, and this was the fact that the Bishop, Edward Stanley, had invited her to stay for a week in his Palace. It was not the singer's acceptance of his invitation which caused raised eyebrows, for she was known to be a lady of unquestionable virtue. It was, rather, the fact that the Bishop was involved, for he was not universally popular.

When he had taken up office some ten years earlier, Bishop Stanley had found the diocese suffering from years of neglect arising from his predecessor's unwillingness to surrender to rapidly advancing senility. Thus it was that he became that most unpopular of men – a reformer. It was not merely the changes he made, but equally the speed and manner in which he set about them. Then there were the little personal peculiarities which his opponents seized upon in order to belittle him. For instance, the fact that he was a bird lover would most probably have been welcomed if only he had not carried it to extremes. It was the rooks which threatened to bring about his downfall.

There had long been a rookery in the great trees which adorned the Close and it was on this rookery that the Bishop cast covetous eyes. He had many well-established trees in the Palace garden but, each spring, the rooks treated them with disdain. This, he felt, called for serious action, for he was determined to have his own private rookery. The method he employed is not recorded, but by some means or other he managed to have some of the nests removed from the trees in the Close and transferred to those in his garden. This action provoked anger among his opponents, who were not beyond bribing young boys to climb the Bishop's trees

Surgical Ward at the Jenny Lind Hospital, Christmas 1908.

and raid his new rookery. The incident also earned for him the nickname of "Jim Crow". It is not surprising, therefore, that, when it became known that he was to play host to Jenny Lind, much merriment was caused by references to "The Nightingale in the Crow's Nest".

This was all very unfortunate, for the strong bond of friendship which later developed between Bishop Edward Stanley and his Swedish guest was destined to bring great benefit to the peoples of both countries. She is on record as having said that it was the Bishop who persuaded her to give up the operatic arena in favour of the concert platform and, when praised for the large sums of money she had raised for charitable purposes, she replied simply, "All this the Bishop of Norwich began in me".

Her place in the affections of the people of Norwich became legendary when, in 1849, she gave two more concerts in the city. Both were attended by capacity audiences and the total sum of £1263 was raised, which she immediately donated to the city for the founding of "some lasting charity for the poor". Even then, Norwich did not appear to be getting the hospital which later bore her name, for the first suggestion was that the money should be spent on public baths to give the people of the city access to an amenity which was not present in their homes. Fortunately,

173

however, the estimated cost of such a facility was found to be almost double the amount of money available. Then it was realised that, by converting a group of houses in Pottergate, a modest little hospital with just a dozen beds could be provided. Thus was born the Jenny Lind Infirmary for Sick Children. There, among the teeming masses of that congested area, the dingy little building offered succour to the deprived until, in 1897, the local proceeds of Queen Victoria's Jubilee Fund were used to erect a bright new building in Unthank Road. Within its walls, still bearing the name of its original benefactor, countless children were restored to health until, more recently, its work was taken over within a tower block of the Norfolk and Norwich Hospital.

That, then, was the story I discovered about the love affair between the City of Norwich and the Swedish Nightingale. Perhaps the most fitting epitaph is to be found in the words of Jenny Lind herself, who wrote, "Of all the money which God allowed me to give away when my poor throat could call an audience to listen to its production, none has borne a nobler or more genuine fruit than the Jenny Lind Hospital of Norwich".

A present-day stroll through the pedestrianised centre of Norwich can be a most pleasurable experience for, as one turns almost every corner, one's ears are treated to a veritable feast of music from instruments of all kinds. I refer not to the cacophony of canned sound which bellows forth through the open doorways of so many of the modern shops (about which, the less said the better), but rather to that of the young musicians who take up their pre-ordained positions at various locations and fill the air with a sweetness of sound which can come only from the artistry of a dedicated performer. The ubiquitous guitar is always there, of course, but so also are the violin and the cello, the flute and the recorder, all in the hands of practised performers who take an obvious pride in their art.

This, of course, is far from being anything new, for there was always music in the streets of Grandma's Norwich. In those Victorian days, however, it must be said that it was of a rather more raucous nature, coming largely from the hurdy gurdy and the barrel organ. There were a few itinerant musicians but it was mostly the organ grinder, with the inevitable little monkey clad in red coat and fez-type hat, who drew the biggest crowds. There was also a host of other characters who sought to make a living in the city streets by other than musical means. Many of them were little more than out-and-out beggars, of whom the most pathetic must surely have been "Little Joe". Wearing threadbare clothing and a doleful expression, he would trudge through the streets singing the one and only song in his repertoire, thus:

> "Poor little Joe, out in the snow;
> Nowhere to shelter, nowhere to go.
> No mother to guide me,
> In the grave she lies low;
> Alone in the wide world
> I'm poor little Joe."

The fact that this was his only offering tended to inject an air of monotony into his performance and, even worse, there were times when the words were singularly inappropriate. In the frost and snow of winter it may have been possible to feel a degree of sympathy for the dejected little figure. In the heat of midsummer, however, with the women dressed in their cotton "washing frocks" and the water cart frantically trying to lay the dust in the scorching city streets, the song tended to lose much of its impact. Then there was the fact that Little Joe was afflicted with a permanent sniffle, and the fact that every few words would be punctuated with one of his sniffs did little to endear him to his audience.

There were, however, other characters who, by dint of sheer personality or what is now known as charisma, earned for themselves not just the affection of the public but, indeed, a permanent place in the annals of the city. Heading the list of such men must surely be the much loved Billy Bluelight.

William Cullum, to give him his proper name, was born in 1859 and, throughout his long life, became such a constant feature of the local scene that there can be few people who did not know him. Indeed, there can be little doubt that he was far better known to the general public than were the men who controlled the city's civic and commercial affairs, and certainly his memory has outlived most of theirs. I knew him only in his later years, but I have heard so much about him from so many people that I have the distinct feeling of having known him throughout his life. "He was always neat and tidy," they said. "He never used bad language and he never lost his temper. And you could see your face in the toes of his boots."

On most summer days he was to be found at his regular station on Gentleman's Walk, just by the entrance to the Royal Arcade, offering for sale sprigs of heather which he had earlier gathered from Felthorpe Woods. "Nature's beauty," he would cry. "Nature's beautiful heather – straight out of Nature's garden." There were many who regarded him as something of a simpleton, but nothing could have been further from the truth. He was well aware that politeness from him and sympathy from passers-by added up to good business. Ladies doing their shopping would pat him on the head and greet him with a cheery "Hello, William." "The well-to-do from Newmarket Road," as one contemporary described them, never failed to thrust a penny into his hand.

There were just two days in every week in the summer when he was missing from his post, and they were the days when the pleasure steamer *Jenny Lind,* laden with day trippers, made the journey to Yarmouth from her mooring near Foundry Bridge. On those days, Billy was an early arrival at Riverside, eagerly greeting the passengers as they made their way aboard and then watching and waving as the steamer set off downstream. Only when she rounded the first bend and disappeared from view would Billy turn his back on the scene. Then he would set off at a steady pace up Thorpe Road to walk the twenty miles to meet her when she arrived at her destination. By the time the *Jenny Lind* reached Yarmouth and tied up at the quayside, Billy would already be there, standing cap-in-hand, ready to receive both their praise and their pence.

Half the money he received would go into his pocket and the other half was set aside for "business purposes". Then he would set off to one of the old Yarmouth Rows, where a certain Mr. Leach engaged in the business of Sweet Boiler, making Yarmouth Rock, boiled sweets and cough sweets. It was the latter of these in which Billy invested, taking them home and packing them away in tins for the winter, when there would be no more heather in Felthorpe Woods and no more day trips on the *Jenny Lind.* Then he would go on his rounds of the city, knocking on doors and offering "Leach's Cough Remedy – Patronised by the Norwich City footballers," and adding, "As the oil is to the machine, so is this wonderful cough remedy to the lungs – my dear old mother personally recommend 'em."

Billy Bluelight in his running gear.

The pleasure boat *Jenny Lind*.

Billy always had a sense of occasion and, whatever he was doing, he always dressed for the part. When selling Leach's Cough Remedy there was always the long, black coat and the black cap with the shiny peak. On Sundays there were the neatly pressed trousers and the top hat. But his best rig of all, I feel, was the athletic gear he donned when he raced the *Jenny Lind* to Yarmouth – the athlete's cap, the white open-necked shirt and the knee-length shorts, making him look for all the world as though he had just walked off the set of "Chariots of Fire". And, as his friends told me, "he was always neat and tidy . . . . and you could see your face in the toes of his boots".

William Cullum died in 1949 at the age of 90.

CHAPTER 17

Pleasures and Pastimes

Every morning for countless years the skies over Norwich would reverberate with the sound of a single gunshot from the Castle walls. It came, however, not from a conventional firearm, but from a metal globe which, from a suspended position, would fall at the appointed time and set off the minor explosion which became known as the "ten o'clock gun". It was just about the only indication that earlier citizens had to indicate the passage of time but, by the thirties, it had become little more than a revered tradition.

Indeed, the only residents who paid it much heed were the vast flocks of pigeons which, as market scavengers, roosted around the Castle walls. Though they had all been born around the battlements and had been in residence there for many generations, they never seemed to get used to it. The sudden shattering of the peace would create panic in their ranks, sending them wheeling into the air in disarray until they felt that the danger had passed, by which time unsuspecting passers-by frequently found themselves heavily bespattered by missiles from above.

Yet the human residents of the city took little notice of the ten o'clock gun, for there was no great obsession with the passage of time in those days. Life, for the most part, went on at a leisurely pace and there always seemed to be ample time for whatever had to be done. Indeed, there was time to do things with a little bit of style, and this was particularly evident in the practice of "eating out". Nowadays we have Hamburger Houses and Pizza Parlours and the many other establishments which are known collectively, I believe, as "fast food outlets". The thirties, however, were very much the age of the Tea Rooms, where one could deal in leisurely manner with a pot of tea and such delights as fairy cakes and orange butterflies, and scones with jam and cream.

Who, indeed, can forget the Scotch Tea Rooms in White Lion Street, where those two dear ladies presided over the proceedings like a pair of devoted nannies? Or Princes, in Castle Street (before the move to Guildhall Hill), where Mr. Pillow specialised in invalid jellies with his matinee teas? Then there was the Belgravia in Bank

Street – even the names seemed to evoke the very spirit of the age. But the jewel in the crown must surely have been the ancient Curat House, built in the 15th century by city sheriff John Curat on the site of the Old Jewry. It later passed into the hands of the Back family who traded there for four centuries until its more recent conversion into shops and its destruction by fire in the early hours of May 31st 1989.

The shops, too, were somehow typically Norwich. We had branches of some of the national concerns, but it was the local names which dominated the scene – names like Curls and Buntings, Garlands, Chamberlins and Bonds. In Magdalen Street there were the Batterbees, father and son, who boasted of the finest selection of clothing in the Eastern Counties, and there was Green's, looking out onto the Haymarket where, at that time, Sir Thomas Browne sat in the middle of a grassy oasis surrounded by trees. And there was the legendary Rumsey Wells, proud to call himself the most expensive cap-maker in the world, while, in her salon in the Royal Arcade, it almost seemed that Madame Pfob had been looking after ladies' hairdressing requirements for centuries.

Then there was the world of entertainment, which offered the people of Norwich everything they desired. The Agricultural Hall had, perhaps, gone into decline, but there was boxing in the Corn Hall and people were still willing to dress up for musical concerts in St. Andrew's Hall. For dancers there were the Lido, the Sampson and Hercules and, now replaced on Prince of Wales Road by a six-storey office block, the Grosvenor Rooms. Above all, it was the heyday of the cinema and, in this respect, we had something of a surfeit of riches, for it was always difficult to choose which of the city's many cinemas would come within our weekly budget. There was the much-loved Haymarket, with John Bee and the mighty Compton organ rising through the floor and providing musical interludes. There was the modern Carlton and, at the other end of the scale, the Empire in Oak Street, one of the last cinemas to accept jam jars for payment and where unsuspecting patrons were liable to be periodically drenched with disinfectant from the sprays wielded by the usherettes. In St. Andrew's there was the Theatre de Luxe, where the main problem was the pronunciation of its name. Some called it "de lew" and others "de lux", so we usually compromised and called it just the T.D.L.

180

It seems that Norwich folk have always had a great capacity for enjoying themselves and certainly the city has never lacked places of entertainment. In the Music Hall era the city had been well to the fore, with an absolute plethora of such places. There was, for instance, the Alhambra in St. Stephen's, on a site which was eventually occupied by Coller's coalyard; there was the Canterbury in Westlegate, where Charles Watling later ran his carrier's business; and in premises now occupied by Lacey and Lincoln's in St. Giles' there was the Vaudeville. The most renowned of all, however, was the Connaught Varieties in Goat Lane, where the entertainment was of a type which has now passed away for ever. There was the chairman with his hammer, the shelves at the back of the seats to hold the glasses of various beverages and, above all, the generally Rabelaisian atmosphere of the proceedings. It was not considered good form to be seen there, and partitions were cunningly devised to prevent people in the cheaper seats from observing the occupants of the more luxurious quarters. Masters did not like the idea of their men contemplating them in their moments of recreation.

Further along St. Giles' stood the Norfolk Hotel where, as a sideline to its normal business, nightly variety shows were held in the hall in the coach yard. Memories of this establishment have long faded into oblivion, but it is a very different story with the new building which eventually replaced it. When it arose from the rubble of its predecessor, its wide, welcoming facade proclaimed it to be the Grand Opera House, a title which it proudly displayed to the world until its dying day. To generations of entertainment-seekers, however, it became the much loved and now sadly mourned Hippodrome.

The Hippodrome became the home of variety in the city and, over the years, a long succession of talented performers graced its stage. Many of the old music hall stars found a new outlet for their offerings, and there are those among us who recall such as Little Tich, Ella Shields, Gertie Gitana and Hetty King. Then, as the years went by, there came Sandy Powell, Lupino Lane, Arthur English and Tommy Trinder. In 1954 Laurel and Hardy drew the crowds, in spite of the fact that their fee (in excess of £1,000) necessitated a sixpenny increase in the admission price.

As the years went by, the changing tastes of the patrons were reflected in the style of entertainment presented. There followed a period of saucy revues, with young ladies posing as human statues,

Laurel and Hardy on stage at the Hippodrome, 1954.

clad in nothing more than a few wisps of strategically placed chiffon. But, all the while, the threat of the cinema was becoming ever stronger and eventually the management decided to make the switch from live entertainment to films. Seven years of faltering attendances brought a return to variety and repertory shows, but the writing was already on the wall. When, in 1958, the decision was made to change the name of the Hippodrome to the Norfolk Playhouse, the letters became larger and more threatening. The public decided that they no longer needed the old place, no matter what name it be given. It closed its doors for the last time and when, after fifty seven years of living history, the building came under the auctioneer's hammer, Tommy Trinder was one of many who went along to pay their last respects. Now, while a constant stream of motorists enters and leaves the multi-storey car park which took its place, the Hippodrome lives on only in fond memory.

But not all our leisure time was spent on indoor pursuits. Sunday band concerts in the parks were free and well-attended whilst, for some, there was the weekly ritual of a tram ride to the City Cemetery. Others boarded the tram going in the opposite direction to the terminus at the Redan, from where they would make the

Norwich Hippodrome – the beginning . . . .

. . . . and the End.

mile-long walk for an afternoon by the riverside at Thorpe Gardens. Norwich folk have always been fond of the Wensum, with a particular affection for the more upper reaches where it wound its way through Heigham to Hellesdon Mill in the stretch which we always knew as the Back River. It was there that the Dolphin Inn (formerly Bishop Hall's summer residence) offered refreshment and relaxation in its riverside gardens, as did the neighbouring Gibraltar and, further upstream, the Gatehouse. It was the Dolphin which was the great magnet, however, for there one could hire a rowing boat or a canoe for the trip up to the mill at Hellesdon.

Rowing on the Back River was as far removed from Henley Regatta as anything could possibly have been. Nobody dressed up for the occasion, and lack of skill as an oarsman was of no great significance. Two pairs of oars could work in four different rhythms, occasionally flying up in the air in a rather impressive impersonation of a demented water beetle, but nobody bothered – it was simply an occasion of sheer, uncomplicated enjoyment.

It was the same with swimming. In those early days the competitive element had not crept in, and people swam simply for fun – or, with a bar of soap, for a bath. There were several swimming baths along the Back River, though one must hasten to add that they were simply short stretches of river furnished with concrete quays, diving boards and little huts for bathers to undress in. There was the Eagle, where many youngsters learned to swim; there was the Dolphin, where bathers were accompanied by the swans which nested on the little island and where the two James Careys, father and son, spent their lives boat-letting and life-saving; and there was the pool where kindly old Mr. Norton, a true Heigham worthy, held court. It was Norton's Baths, in fact, which became the site of the Swan Baths under the direction of the old man's son-in-law, William Ransome.

It was here that, as early as 1879, Norwich had its first indoor heated swimming pool when the enterprising Swan Laundry used some of its spare steam for the purpose. And it was there that, the following year, a group of youthful Victorians (including William Ransome and James Carey from the Dolphin) got together to form the club which has now been part of the city's history for over a century.

Much emphasis was placed on life-saving instruction in those early days, for the river was not without its hidden dangers for the

Billy Basher giving life-saving instruction at the Eagle Baths, 1926.

unwary. The examinations of the Royal Life Saving Society were held in the river rather than in the pleasant conditions of heated baths, and Reggie Mace, for many years a star of the local swimming firmament, recalls the contrast: "If the river was in full spate", he said, "there was quite a tide running and to tow a patient in those conditions and pass the Bronze or Silver Medals you had to be an expert".

Toughness and physical strength likewise played a big part in the sport of water polo, which also figured highly in the club's activities. There seemed to be no shortage of well-rounded figures amongst the male members and, indeed, there was one particular season when the club could surely have claimed to have had the heaviest team in England, with the seven members providing a combined weight of 105 stones. Charlie "Tiny" Gaskin got them off to a good start, for he tipped the scales at something over twenty stones. Then there were the likes of Les "Tank" Roberts, Frank Horsley, "Wrestler" Baker and his equally physical brother, not forgetting C.A. Bulman and Alfred Howell, the captain. At an average weight of fifteen stones, one cannot help thinking that the water level in the pool must have risen quite a few inches when they all got in together.

The heavyweight Norwich Swan water polo team of 1932. Left to right. Back row:
S.J. Baker, C. Bulman, W.J. Basher, F. Horsley, H.J. Baker.
Front row: C. Gaskin, A.G. Howell (capt.), L.R. Roberts.

Norwich Regatta at Whitlingham Reach, 1908.

It was through water polo that, as a small boy, I met Billy Basher, who was to become the great legendary figure of the Swan Swimming Club. My father, though not boasting the massive proportions of the aforementioned seven, played in one of the teams and it was when I went to give him my support that I was introduced to the bespectacled little man who became "Mr. Swan". Nobody did more for the club than Billy, and it was a cruel stroke of fate that he should die so close to the realisation of his great dream of an indoor swimming pool in the city. Now he has become one of the great memories of local swimming – memories stretching back to the days when hardy souls made their way to the Back River to be confronted with frosty diving boards and ice-covered waters which had to be broken to enable a certain local dentist to take his pre-breakfast plunge.

The undemanding simplicity of those early exploits on the Back River was also reflected at holiday times, for it was an age when nobody except the rich and famous went abroad for their holidays, and few of us came into either of those categories. Thus, the sum total of our holiday destinations by the time I was fifteen consisted merely of Hemsby, Sea Palling and a week in a boarding house at Yarmouth.

A bungalow at Hemsby was our regular August mecca, and there we would spend a blissful fortnight, though the place itself had nothing more to offer than sand, sea, sun – and Mr. Olley's shop down in the Gap. The great thing was that the same families occupied the same bungalows during the same weeks of every year and thus a bond of friendship grew up between us. The highlight of every day was the evening cricket match in the valley between the marram hills, with as many as twenty players in each team and everybody fielding. Then, when bad light brought a halt to the proceedings, we would converge on the Gap like a herd of lemmings, with Mr. Olley acknowledging our arrival with mixed feelings. He welcomed the thought of doing a modest amount of business but, at the same time, he was like a soul in torment when we gathered round his horse-racing machine. It was supposed to be a money-spinner for the owner, with only one chance in eight of winning, but we had probed its innermost secrets and found its Achilles Heel. Hard though he tried, he never solved the mystery of our hundred per cent success rate. To be fair, however, we always spent our winnings in his shop, so his turnover increased even if his profits did not quite follow the same pattern.

My one holiday sojourn at Sea Palling was spent in a similarly idyllic fashion, though it was not without its moments of trauma. The big difference was that I had been invited to share the holiday with my aunt and my four cousins and, much as I loved them all, it was the first time I had stayed away from the bosom of my immediate family. Thus it was that, within twenty four hours, I suffered, for the first time, the painful pangs of homesickness. So bad was it, in fact, that, by the time my mother came down to pay us a midweek visit, I had already packed my little case ready to go home with her. I was prevailed upon to stay, however, and I have always been glad that I did, in spite of one other moment of crisis which arose later in the week.

We were staying in a fisherman's cottage and, although we found it pleasurably cosy, it was not exactly over-endowed with modern facilities. At nightfall, our lighting in the parlour came from a paraffin lamp, and we took a candle to light our way up the stairs to bed. This was all great fun, but the same could not be said about the sanitary arrangements. At home, we had become accustomed to flush toilets, but here the only facilities were sited within a little wooden hut at the bottom of the long, winding path down through the vegetable garden. Even this was not too bad during daylight hours but, as darkness fell, our minds became filled with thoughts of all sorts of monsters lurking among the vegetables on either side of the path. Thus, Aunt Laura introduced a routine under which, before we retired to our beds, we would all gather together and, with lighted candle held aloft, she would lead us down to the little hut. Then, having each taken our turn, we would make the return trip, with the potato patch on one side and the Jerusalem artichokes on the other, under the rose-covered arch and back to the safety of the lamplit parlour.

The system worked extremely well until the fateful night when one of our number (who shall remain nameless) missed the nightly convoy. The result was that, during the course of the night, there was a somewhat unfortunate occurrence, over the details of which I propose to draw a veil, other than to say that dear Aunt Laura was very understanding.

Looking back over the years, I can only marvel at the degree of happiness which we found in those early childhood weeks by the sea. Yet, even now, I find it difficult to recall any more recent and more adventurous holiday which brought with it a greater feeling of sheer, unsophisticated pleasure.

CHAPTER 18

No Regrets.

Norfolk is all things to all people. I count myself three times blessed in that I was born by the seaside, raised in the country and brought into manhood in the city. Perhaps the fact that, when the war was over, I chose to put down my roots in the countryside will indicate where my true love lies. I am fond of Norwich but I feel much more at peace with the world in a country lane than on a city street.

And, of course, it was in the country that those first little snippets of memory began assembling themselves in the back of my mind. Such things as going off to Infants' School with a big hand-kerchief pinned to my smock, and wearing leather gaiters in the cold weather, with the anguish of having all those little buttons done up with a button-hook. Wearing a scarf and mittens in class during the hard days of winter, with Miss Rump warming her ample posterior in front of the stove so that none of its heat reached us. The joy of the magic lantern, with its pictures of A Storm in the Bay of Biscay, Mount Vesuvius Erupting, and Napoleon (or was it Hannibal?) Crossing the Alps.

There was shopping with my mother and watching the change come hurtling back on the overhead railway; the excitement of Christmas, with "Chatterbox" and "Tiger Tim's Annual" in my stocking; and Sunday afternoon picnics on Felmingham Heath. Then, as the years went by, there was the hero-worship of such men as Jack Hobbs and Malcolm Campbell, not to mention winding up the gramophone and listening to Deanna Durbin records.

It always seemed to be a time when nothing ever changed, and yet, in retrospect, one becomes aware that developments were taking place all the time. There was nothing as dramatic as man walking on the Moon or of being able to fire a missile which could hit an unseen target a continent away. But there was wireless, and I well recall the sight of my older brother, earphones on his head, twiddling with the cat's whisker on our crystal set so that my father could hear the election results. Then came the sets powered by an accumulator, with the necessity for making sure that there was a spare one in the cupboard when the first one had to go to the ironmonger for recharging. Finally came the luxury of the All-Mains Wireless Set, bringing with it that air of reverence as Stuart Hibberd read the news and the almost uncontrollable excitement as Radio Luxembourg gave us the Ovaltineys, the Betox Brigade and Big Bill Campbell broadcasting to us from the Old Log Cabin.

Then, of course, there was the telephone, and I believe it was this innovation which made the greatest impact on our household, for the bell did not ring with the dulcet tones of today's models. When it demanded attention in those early days, it was like a fire engine driving madly through the house and, as my mother so often said, it was "enough to waken the dead". Then there was the special voice which everybody adopted when speaking on the new machine. Each syllable was enunciated with an exaggerated clarity which bore no resemblance to normal speech, and I recall more than one occasion when, on hearing a strange voice in the hall, I peered round the banisters to see who the visitor was and discovered that it was merely Father on the 'phone.

So, were they really the good old days? I certainly believe that we had a greater understanding of the meaning of true contentment, but I will go no further than that. It is not simply that our lives have changed since those years between the wars, but rather that we now live in a totally different world. Thus, comparisons would be not only odious but also futile. It would be like trying to compare a Gainsborough with a Picasso or Concorde with a Tiger Moth. Hence, I lay aside my rose-tinted spectacles and merely acknowledge my good fortune in having grown to manhood in those now far-distant days. In the words of Edith Piaf, there are no regrets.